Believe

SAM FROST

WITH KRISTINE ROSS

Believe

hachette AUSTRALIA

IMPORTANT NOTE TO READERS: This book details the personal experiences of the authors and must not be treated as a substitute for qualified medical advice. Always consult a qualified medical practitioner. Neither the authors nor the publisher can be held responsible for any loss or claim arising out of the use, or misuse, of the suggestions made or the failure to take professional advice.

Published in Australia and New Zealand in 2022
by Hachette Australia
(an imprint of Hachette Australia Pty Limited)
Gadigal Country, Level 17, 207 Kent Street, Sydney, NSW 2000
www.hachette.com.au

Hachette Australia acknowledges and pays our respects to the past, present and future Traditional Owners and Custodians of Country throughout Australia and recognises the continuation of cultural, spiritual and educational practices of Aboriginal and Torres Strait Islander peoples. Our head office is located on the lands of the Gadigal people of the Eora Nation.

A catalogue record for this book is available from the National Library of Australia

ISBN: 978 0 7336 4751 2 (paperback)

Cover design by Christabella Designs
Cover photograph by Sam Frost
Authors photograph courtesy Kristine Ross
Typeset in Sabon LT Std by Kirby Jones
Printed and bound in Australia by McPherson's Printing Group

The paper this book is printed on is certified against the Forest Stewardship Council® Standards. McPherson's Printing Group holds FSC® chain of custody certification SA-COC-005379. FSC® promotes environmentally responsible, socially beneficial and economically viable management of the world's forests.

For our angels Paul and Pete; Mum; brothers,
Steve, Jeff, Alex and Josh; sister, Kristine. And Dave.
Thank you for your unwavering support and love.
I'm forever grateful.
Sam

For my beautiful girls, Bridie and Olive. You are my
everything. Love Mum xx
Kristine

Contents

BODY

SPIRIT

Introduction

You've probably seen articles in magazines and online where people are asked to give a piece of advice to their younger selves. There are a few things we could advise, but there's actually only one main thing I would tell my younger self: while it may not seem like it right now, it is a blessing to face hardship. The challenges you endure only make you stronger, wiser, kinder, more empathetic, and they help you appreciate the small things in life. They make you believe in yourself. They make you believe and trust that everything has a purpose. That there is a lesson to be learnt. Had you never lived in complete darkness, you wouldn't appreciate the light.

I believe one of my greatest gifts is empathy. My ability to feel the story I hear as though it happened to me. It helps me feel connected to the world around me, to the humans I meet. The downside of this beautiful gift of human and worldly connection is that I also feel pain and sadness just as deeply.

I don't claim to know all the answers; most of the time I'm still figuring it out myself. But what I can do is share an insight into the challenges I've faced that stem from depression, anxiety, social media, toxic relationships, body image issues, and grief. I can offer you tips that have helped me find the light when darkness is all that I could see. I've had my fair share of battles, and I still believe in the good in the world. I still have faith. I still have my sense of humour, my kindness, my empathy, my compassion, and my deep trust in the universe. I believe that I'm on a journey of self-discovery, of growth and evolution, and I want you to come on the journey with me. Hopefully my story will help you believe in all the beauty that life has to offer.

•

When I first wake up in the morning I always have an hour to myself. I have a cup of coffee and then I sit in complete stillness. I have had this ritual since I was a teenager, and I don't know why; I've just intuitively done it. When I was a teen I didn't think of this habit as a form of meditation or mindfulness, although now I realise it is. And it has become a fundamental part of my daily routine.

Each day during this time of stillness, which can be from 45 minutes to an hour, I really think about how I'm feeling. I try to sit back within myself and see my thoughts and emotions objectively and try to connect the dots as to why I'm feeling a certain way. I think about what I need to do for the day, and I always try to reconnect to myself to feel centred and aligned. I feel as though the answer to life's questions can always be found in the stillness. It's my time for me. I feel like that is the most important time I have to myself.

With filming *Home and Away*, sometimes I have to be up at 4 a.m. to make it to set on time. On those days I will get up at 3 a.m. to ensure I have my hour. I always have to make time for myself, no matter how early it is or where I am or how packed the day ahead may be.

Then each night – and this is a very, very new thing – I journal.

Recently I was meditating at night, writing in my journal, and I told myself, 'Tomorrow is going to be a magical day. It's going to be a beautiful day filled with miracles.' I went to bed feeling hopeful and at peace.

The next day was one of the worst days of my life. I received some heartbreaking news. I just cried and cried and cried. Then I went to my friend Katy's house and continued to cry hysterically, 'I asked for a magical day and these awful things happened instead!'

We chatted for hours, about how I felt like I had lost my faith in the universe. Lost the hopeful spark that keeps me excited about life. My friend was kind and held space for me to vent my frustrations and the injustice I felt. Then she said, 'Mate, it's going to get better because the odds are in your favour.' And I just burst out laughing. We continued to joke and find the humour in my situation. I was giggling to myself the entire way home.

That night I sat on my bed, looked at my journal and thought, *I asked for a magical day! Yet you set off every single trigger I have!* I started to get mad again. I was exhausted from holding on to hope. I didn't think there was any purpose in staying hopeful – it only sets you up to be disappointed. But then, in the stillness, I thought about all the good things that had happened during the day. All the tiny miracles. I realised there was still so much beauty and magic in the world.

I thought about how I had changed. I reflected on what I used to be like. If I had received those knocks six months beforehand, I would have been knocked down and out. That would have set me off on another depressive state for a week. Instead, I picked up the phone, called a friend, reached out to someone.

I never used to reach out. I'd isolate myself, hide in a hole, turn my phone off, shut out the world. But I ended up laughing with Katy about how weird and how unfair life is sometimes. I felt grateful to be surrounded by beautiful friends, who love me unconditionally through the good, bad and very ugly. It was a day of self-reflection and a day where I found magic, gratitude and humour instead of being crippled into depression.

I realised I have grown. I have evolved. All the work I put into myself by practising mindfulness and meditation, seeing a psychologist regularly, working through the trauma and becoming aware, and accountable – look how far I've come. I'm no longer a victim of my past. I am **free**.

Which is pretty magical to me.

•

There's no trick to growth; there are no shortcuts. It took me years of work, and it still takes work. There will always be awful days that might derail me and I need to try my best to make sure they don't. Because nothing is more important than my health – specifically, my mental health.

I know there are a lot of you who are having awful days, who are struggling right now while you're reading this. I can't take your pain away, but I can hold your hand and walk through this terrain with you. Some of you send me messages – messages from the heart, messages containing your truth. You trust me with your pain. That is an extraordinary privilege. It's not one I take for granted – *ever.* It's also the reason why my sister, Kristine, and I established our online community, BELIEVE by Sam Frost.

I feel a great responsibility towards the people who write to me. I think having a career in the public eye means I have a responsibility to be a good role model, to be authentic and to help where I can.

One of the main reasons we created BELIEVE was because I was inundated with people reaching out to me, sharing stories of their struggles. I'm a very empathetic person, so I don't just surface-read them, I feel them. I am deeply humbled and appreciative of the people who have gone out of their way to be vulnerable, to share raw stories, to share parts of their lives with a stranger. I think it takes a great deal of bravery and courage.

After talking to women and teenagers through BELIEVE and its sister organisation, Stronger – by BELIEVE, I realised there was more to say. I wanted to share more of my story. I think you will see some of yourself in me, just as I've seen myself in some in you.

What's in these pages are the things I would want to say to you if you were to write to me. Stories about my own life to help you navigate yours, and things I've learnt on the way.

That's one of the reasons why I've written this book.

Another is that I'm a massive book lover. I love having something on my bookshelf that I can always open when I feel like I need guidance, some advice or reassurance that I'm not alone. I hope *Believe* can be that for you. I wanted to create something that people can have in their homes that they can go to when they feel like they're lost or need guidance. Hopefully this book will help you feel confident and like you're less alone and, more importantly, help you find yourself, find hope and light.

One of my favourite books – and it's a classic for a reason – is *The Alchemist* by Paulo Coelho. I think it's such a beautiful book about trusting your intuition and how even when there are detours in life, they always end up leading you to exactly where you are meant to be. Anytime I face challenges or difficulties I always just trust that this is happening for a reason and, ultimately, I'm exactly where I need to be. *The Alchemist* always reminds me of that. I hope *Believe* is the start of a conversation you have not just with me but with yourself.

I want you to believe in yourself. I *know* there is so much about you that you can believe in. If you're not sure, I hope this book will help you become sure. It may be the first step in your journey to self-belief or perhaps it's one of the steps along the way. Maybe you're reading it just because you're curious. Whatever the reason, if this book helps in even just a tiny way, then I feel it's done its job.

Throughout this book you'll see sections written by my sister, Kristine. She is going to give you some great information and helpful advice – the sort of advice she gives me. Kristine is the Founder and Director of Stronger – by BELIEVE. She is a youth mentor, children's yoga teacher and workshop facilitator, as well as the mother of two daughters. Kris has spent a lot of time thinking about how to make life better for other people and putting it into practice. I trust her completely and I know you can trust her too.

What you're also going to see in the following pages are some stories from me, and some information that can help if you've been in a similar position. The details of my stories may not match the details of yours, but I bet the *feeling* in them does. It's because I know that we're not all that different to each other, you and me, and I'm prepared to tell my story in the hope that it helps you on the bad days as well as the good – and the days that are a mix of both. Mostly we don't know when stresses will arise or challenges will surface, but we usually need something to help us get right when they do. I hope this book can be that for you. So here goes.

Mind

It's been said over and over again, by many different people, because it's true: mental health is as important as physical health. The difficulty a lot of us have with maintaining our mental health, and seeking help when we're having mental health challenges, is that we can't *see* it the way we can see problems with our physical health. A broken bone is easily diagnosed and if you're wearing a cast everyone knows what's happened. But if your mind feels broken there's not an easy way to show people that you're in pain and you need care. Sometimes we don't show it until we are way past the point of needing help; we needed that help earlier but either didn't know how to access it or felt too ashamed to ask.

I have been open about my challenges with mental health. The website I created with my sister, Kristine, is focused on mental health. It's called BELIEVE by Sam Frost, like this book, because that concept underpins so much of my own work on my mental wellbeing. I believe in myself. I believe that I can always improve the state of my mind. And I believe in you and your ability to improve your mental health, if that's what you need or want to do.

I am not a medical expert; I do not have a degree in anything. But I'm an expert in my own mental health, and I have experiences and knowledge that I believe will help you. Because we're all here on this planet doing our best, even if some days are so much harder than others. I've had those sorts of days. I'll have them again. So will you. But when we believe in ourselves we start to change our mindset, and that means we can start to manage those bad days better and, eventually, have fewer of them.

Dark places

I've been there. Where you are. Or where you've been. Where you might find yourself one day. *That place.* That dark place we can all go to.

Sometimes the pain is so unbearable I can't stand the thought of being in my own body anymore. I just want to sleep the days away. I'll keep the curtains shut and hide in darkness.

But something I always try to remind myself of is that I'm exactly where I'm meant to be. Sometimes I will be crying and saying to myself, 'I know that this is supposed to be happening for a reason but I'm *tired*.' Or I know that I'm supposed to be learning a lesson and I think, *Okay, I've learnt enough lessons now – can we just get things moving and back on track?*

Ultimately, though, I truly believe that even during difficulties and even through the darkness, this is supposed to be happening for whatever reason, and I'm going to grow from it and learn from it. Maybe that's just a coping mechanism – but even if it is, it works.

Once I get through the darkness I ask myself, 'What did I learn and how did I change in a positive way?' and, always, there has been a positive change. *Always.* But it can be hard to see that when you're in the midst of it.

This is something that I've only been able to put into practice over the last couple of years, since I turned 30. In the past, I would have moments after huge challenges or adversity, or whatever it may be, when I'd say, 'What did I learn?' Nowadays I do this for any bad days that I have and not just for huge events.

In other words, I haven't had it all sorted out for my whole life. In fact, I still don't have it all sorted out. But I've learnt some things that helped me and may help you too.

In my twenties I had to try to switch the way I was thinking because the way I perceived things was really unhelpful to me. I used to think about my life and it didn't make sense to me why so many bad things kept happening and I just kept getting knocked and knocked and knocked. My whole life had been a series of different knocks. I would get blown down for days and weeks and months, and then I'd get back up and think, *Okay, cool, I got through it.* Then something would happen to knock me down again, followed by another thing, and I felt like I was constantly being challenged and facing difficulties in my life. It didn't make sense to me, because I felt like I was a good person.

I remember once when I was working on radio and I was fielding a lot of criticism. I felt like I just couldn't catch a break, and I remember I said – and I think I said it publicly – 'I don't understand because I'm a good person and I try to do the right thing and I'm always kind to people, and I'm generous with my time and my energy, and I feel like I'm a person who chooses kindness always.'

You know what? That way of thinking did not help me at all. No matter how many times I told myself that I didn't deserve to have bad things happen to me, it did not stop them happening. In fact, I became really depressed because I just felt like, well, it doesn't matter what I do anyway because it's not going to work out for me.

That's the phrase I would use: *it's not going to work out for me.* It's actually only in the past few months (at the time of writing) that I've realised, with the help of my psychologist, that I kept telling myself this phrase. *Only months ago!* Thinking and saying 'What's the point because it's not going to work out for me' had become a pattern. A damaging pattern. It's something that I want to try to change now and I have to figure out how to do that. I'm still working on it.

I'm sharing this with you as a way of showing you that even after we learn a lot about ourselves we can continue to discover new things, and that those discoveries can be useful. No doubt I'll discover a new lesson to learn soon and that will be another step on my path in the right direction. Because this work is never done. There's no 'ending' because our lives are always full of change. You may think you have one thing sorted then something happens to you – something you can't control – and it can feel like you've gone backwards. That's why we just keep putting one foot in front of the other: so we can progress. Even if there's no end to the road, it's important to keep moving forwards.

As an example: I would not have arrived where I am now, working on changing this damaging pattern of thinking, if I hadn't faced up to the way I was thinking in my twenties. The skills I need to make positive change now are skills I've learnt over the course of my life. In my mid-twenties I ended up having to change the way I thought, otherwise I was going to be depressed my entire life. That was not how I wanted to live.

That's when I thought, *Obviously I'm being taught lessons – what are they?* I had to start practising mindfulness and meditation and really try to feel centred and connected to who I am, and see the bigger picture. It was just not going to work out for me if I hadn't changed the way I thought. It still wouldn't. It never will.

So I keep going. Plodding along sometimes, skipping down the road other times. People around me use the word 'resilient' a lot. Anytime I'm low they say, 'You're the most resilient person I know.' Sometimes I respond by saying, 'I'm tired of being resilient!'

Recently one of my brothers said to me, 'Just be strong', and I said, 'I'm tired of being strong! It's exhausting!'

Some days I feel more resilient than other days. But ultimately I have this commitment to myself – and I've always had it in me: I want to learn and grow and evolve. I constantly want to keep working on myself, forever and ever and ever, because I want to have the best life I possibly can, be the best version of myself, and know that I've done everything I can to achieve this.

There's this saying, which you've probably heard before, but I really believe it: *Choose your hard*. It's something that I think about often. Because when I'm down and out, and when I'm going through my depression, I'll be in my bed in a dark room for days, and I won't have energy to even go downstairs to eat. I won't have energy to do anything and I don't want to move. I'm just still.

It's hard staying in bed all day. It's hard going through depression. It's hard because you're sad and your body hurts and your heart hurts. But what's also hard is getting out of bed and taking steps to be healthier. Taking small steps like having breakfast, having a shower. So if that's what you've done for the day, that's good enough. Staying in the darkness or getting up, either one is hard, but you have to think,

Which is the hard that's going to be the most beneficial for me? For me, that is getting out of bed, having a shower, eating, calling my sister, and actually taking those steps towards a better day.

This principle applies to any situation that knocks you down. When you're in a relationship that doesn't make you happy, it's hard staying in that and it's also hard leaving – but which one is the most beneficial for your health and your happiness? So I always think about *choosing my hard* when I'm making decisions.

When people are sharing their experiences with me, I connect to their story and feel everything that they feel. Which is beautiful, because it means I have wonderful friends and powerful connections with people. But it also means that I feel *everything*, and it is hard when people who are trying to help me come out of the darkness say, 'You should be strong!'

I want to say, 'You don't even know.'

That's the thing about depression that makes it so isolating: only you can know what it feels like to be in your body at that time, and no matter what anyone else says, you're thinking, *You don't know what this feels like. You don't get it.*

The truth is no one does get it. People go through their own versions of mental health struggles, but no one knows in that moment in time how you're feeling in your body, in your mind and in your heart.

So when people say to you, 'Just be strong! Just choose to be happy! Just get out of bed! Don't worry about it!' – all those classic things – it actually doesn't help. If anything, I think it makes you feel more alone and more likely to hide away because you think, *They don't get it. The world doesn't get it. I'm just going to stay in here.* It's really important for people to be mindful of what they're saying, of how they're supporting their loved ones when they're in a dark place. If you find yourself in this situation, instead of saying what you think someone should do to feel better – which implies a judgement of how they're feeling – acknowledge where they are and let them know you're there to support them. A phrase as simple as 'What can I do to support you?' says so much and contains no pressure to 'be happy' or 'not worry'. (Please also see Kristine's section 'Being the support person' on page 124.)

There is one way it does help, though. If, for example, my brothers are worried about me, regardless of what they're saying I can tell that they're feeling helpless – so then I know I have to put my feet on the ground and try to go on for them. Because the helplessness that they feel is painful for me to see and I know it's painful for them to see their sister struggling.

I guess a lot of my resilience comes from faking it until I make it, and thinking, *Well, I'd better do this for them.* I get back up and do it – put one foot in front of the other – for my brothers and for my sister and for my family. As a result people say, 'You're so resilient!' but I'm not really. I'm just doing it for them so they stop worrying about me. While making better choices for ourselves is a very important skill to master, doing something that is for the benefit of other people is as valid a reason as any.

Just to paint a picture of my family – I have two big brothers, Steve and Jeff, and two little brothers, Alex and Josh; Kristine and I are in the middle. Jeff, who I speak to quite regularly – we FaceTime often – is so kind and so beautiful and has the best heart, but he doesn't say much. He's exactly what a truck driver is assumed to be! His part of our conversations is: 'Righto, mate. Yep. Nup.' So you have to join the dots to work out what he's really saying. My brothers express their care through the action of calling, even if they don't say much at all, which they don't. If you have family members like this too, they will probably have the best intentions in the world about wanting to talk to you, but don't be surprised if you don't get much more than I do out of Jeff! They're showing their love and support by reaching out. And sometimes that's all we need from people.

ULTIMATELY I HAVE THIS COMMITMENT TO MYSELF — AND I'VE ALWAYS HAD IT IN ME: I WANT TO LEARN AND GROW AND EVOLVE.

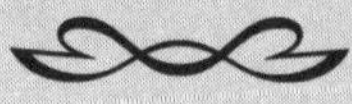

Mental fitness

I have taken responsibility for my mental health. Part of the reason for me talking about it in this book is that I want to encourage others to take care of their mental health too. It's no different to taking responsibility for your physical health. No one else can go to the gym for you to maintain your fitness (even if you wish they could!) and no one else can do the work to keep you mentally fit. Yes, you can engage professionals to give you guidance but you can't look to anyone outside of yourself to do that maintenance work.

Maintaining my mental fitness has always been something I'm conscious of and that is because my beautiful mum struggles with mental illness. I'll be honest and say that looking after my mental health started off as an obsession with the idea that I didn't want to have the same struggles as she does. Now that I've worked with my psychologist and healed that deep fear, I know that one of the most important things you can do as a human being is look after your mental health.

I look after my physical health – I eat well, I'm active. I think we need to look after our minds just as much, if not more. Also I want to be mentally fit when I'm older. The days that I waste feeling down and out – I don't want to live my entire life like that. Instead, I want to maintain this commitment to myself to constantly learn, grow and evolve, which primarily is looking after my mental health and healing the things that need to heal.

Of course, there are always people who don't take responsibility for their physical and mental health and if you are not one of those people, you probably get very annoyed with them, like I do. That's not to say that I don't understand that there are reasons why someone may not be able to – or want to, at that point in their life – take responsibility for themselves.

Sometimes it's because they think they don't deserve to have better physical or mental health, or for reasons that are beyond their control. I can relate to that.

I once worked with someone who was constantly miserable and grumpy and angry. I said to him, 'Mate, you are a miserable person.' His response was, 'Sam, this is who I am.' And that drove me mad because that attitude affected the entire workplace. My take was 'you're deciding this is who you are, so your whole schtick is this miserable, grumpy person who's angry about everything.' How exhausting this must be!

But by then I was in a space where other people's negative energies didn't affect me, which was very freeing. I felt so liberated and empowered.

You can feel the negativity when people like that enter a room. They bring the energy down. Similarly, you can feel when someone enters a room with beautiful energy and lifts the energy of others. That's the type of person I want to be and I like to think it's the type of person I am. And that's because I'm self-aware and I'm conscious of how I'm feeling and how it impacts other people.

I do get frustrated, though. I get frustrated if people behave badly and they say, 'Oh well – that's who I am.' That mentality makes me really cross. Because if you want to, you can change it. It's really, really hard and you have to be dedicated and committed to yourself. But some people don't want to – or can't – change and I just think, *Well, that's unfortunate because you could feel so happy and have a beautiful life.*

I also think it's a bit rude for someone to shrug and say, 'That's just me', when their behaviour affects everyone around them. I prefer to make sure I'm in the best possible shape mentally so I'm not adversely impacting other people. It takes work, and commitment; I know that you may not be in the place yet where you can make the same commitment, but I also know that caring about the impact I am having on other people really helps me. It gives me a focus, and a goal. So I'm here to encourage you to try the same, and also to stand up for yourself in situations where someone's behaviour is having a negative impact on you.

Sometimes it's not enough, and you can't change people. But that doesn't mean you have to put up with their behaviour or change yourself to suit them.

How to build and maintain mental fitness
BY KRISTINE

Take some time out for YOU each day – all you need is 10 minutes. Find a quiet space that has no distractions (this includes being away from your devices and/or children) to just sit and breathe. The breath is like a mirror of how we feel. Through conscious breathing we can change our tension into relaxation. Also, when you sit in stillness I invite you to just be with the sensations within your body. Notice what comes up for you. (To begin with, this exercise can be hard but I invite you to give it a go and see if you notice a difference in how you feel.)

Be kind to yourself. Give yourself a compliment. Write it down, say it out loud, look yourself in the mirror and say it!

Spark joy in your life. Do something you love every single day!

Journal. Journalling is a fantastic tool for improving your mental health (and for more on this see the section on Journalling on page 44).

Move your gorgeous body. You could put on your favourite song and dance around your room for five minutes, or go for a walk so you can have the benefit of moving *and* being outside in nature. This doesn't need a big time commitment. Even a few minutes are better than none.

Speak with a therapist or counsellor.

Spend time in nature.

Practise self-care. Remember to put yourself first every day and the rest will fall into place.

Practise gratitude. Appreciate the little things. (For more on this see the section on Gratitude on page 248.)

And ... **forgive yourself.** Let go of all your mistakes from the past. They're done, they're over. Stop holding on and forgive yourself.

NO ONE ELSE CAN GO TO THE GYM FOR YOU TO MAINTAIN YOUR FITNESS (EVEN IF YOU WISH THEY COULD!) AND NO ONE ELSE CAN DO THE WORK TO KEEP YOU MENTALLY FIT.

Embracing it all

I remember I said to my psychologist once, 'When I am going to stop being so sad? When am I going to stop feeling things so deeply?'

She said to me, 'Sam, the other part of your personality is that you're a really happy-go-lucky person and you're excitable and you feel joy and you appreciate small things.' And she was right. I'm often in a state of excitement and happiness, I'm silly and playful, and there's a huge part of my personality that's bright and bubbly and colourful, so I feel the highs just as much as I feel the lows. It's a package deal.

She asked me, 'Would you take away your happiness, that excitable part of your personality, if it took away your sadness?'

I said, 'No, I wouldn't, because I love that part of myself.'

Then she explained that I can't have one part without the other. When I feel things deeply during those lows, I remind myself that I feel the highs just as deeply and I think, *I wouldn't have that if I didn't have this.*

My psychologist also said, 'I think you're always going to be like this. This is part of who you are, that you feel things deeply.' The light *and* the dark. Now I've come to realise that this part of my personality actually helps me with my work as an actor and it helps me connect to people.

I have to keep reminding myself about that, though. One thing that I've been struggling with lately is that I feel guilt for how I've treated someone in the past. I'm struggling to feel like I deserve to be treated well because I treated someone else poorly. So then I ruin my day because I'm thinking about something I did four years ago – all of a sudden it has popped into my head. These things just pop up and keep popping up.

You know that arcade game where the little moles pop up and you have to try to whack their heads down? Sometimes I feel like that with problems with mental health. Sometimes I'll think, *Phew, everything seems under control.* Then a random thought will show up about my childhood or relationships or a time I've been humiliated and it'll feel exactly like playing that game. I'm just trying to whack all these thoughts and tell them, 'Stay down there!' while also trying to make things better.

I do think I am particularly hard on myself. I like who I am and I think I'm a kind person and I know that I'm a good friend, too. But I do have moments where I think, *I could have been better in that situation*, or, *I judged this one too quickly.* But I also hold myself accountable because I believe that there's such a power in being responsible for your own behaviour.

Sometimes, though, I take that too far. I have struggled to let things go. If I haven't been the best version of myself in a particular situation or I haven't handled things the best I possibly could, sometimes I hang onto that for too long and it can be detrimental to living in the present. That's something I'm actively working on, staying present, because I can spend so long focusing on how I should've been better in the past or what might happen in the future that I completely miss what's going on right now. It zaps the fun out of my life. Sometimes when I should be having a great time with friends or family, I get so caught up focusing on the past or the future that I'm not present at all.

That all comes about, though, because I want to be the best version of myself – I spend time reflecting on the past so I can learn, and I think about the future so I can prepare. But that means that I will be too hard on myself sometimes. I forget that as a human being, I am always capable of making mistakes when I do things. I do think being tough on myself always comes from a good place though.

I don't think there are any quick fixes to our problems. I've been working with a psychologist for years – since I was 25. I'm constantly working on my mental health. There's always stuff that we can work on. Not to say that the work I'm doing on myself is not helping – of course it's helping. It's making me become wiser and more self-aware and more mindful. When

I do have feelings of anxiety or depression, it makes it easier to manage them. Those feelings don't last as long. They are nowhere near as painful. But I certainly still feel these things, and that's part of who I am – and I don't think that's ever going to change.

I DON'T THINK THERE ARE ANY QUICK FIXES TO OUR PROBLEMS. I'M CONSTANTLY WORKING ON MY MENTAL HEALTH. THERE'S ALWAYS STUFF THAT WE CAN WORK ON.

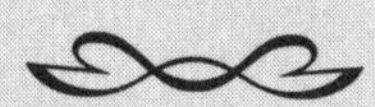

loving yourself well

I've mentioned that I focus on the things that are brilliant about me. Some people can find this language uncomfortable. I recently had a conversation with a girlfriend of mine about this – how I feel that sometimes people don't know how to respond when you're confident or when you like yourself. I find this deeply problematic – and I'll talk more about it in the next chapter.

I know I have a long way to go, but since I've turned 30 the way I've seen myself has changed dramatically. In my teens and twenties, I used to beat myself up constantly, in all areas of my life. I wasn't good enough, pretty enough, smart enough, successful enough. I was just never enough. This deep insecurity and feeling gross and uncomfortable in my own body affected my confidence, my relationships, my friendships and my work.

It was not good at all for me and I just didn't want to live my life like that anymore. It's tiring. I don't want to feel insecure. I don't want to have to wear baggy clothes because I'm unhappy about my body. I don't want to look at myself and hate myself. That's exhausting and a complete waste of energy and time.

I shifted in my thirties – particularly when I was single again. I changed the way I think about myself and instead of beating myself up, I thought, *I'm a survivor.* I started to focus on all the good things about me. I'm wise, funny, smart, kind, silly and playful. Changing our perspective on ourselves and learning to love who we are is something we can all do, though it may feel difficult to start the process.

Recently I attended a mindfulness class. It involved sitting in silence and we were asked to think about who we are at our core – who is that person and what do you like about them? I thought, *I like that I'm grounded, I have many layers, I'm a good listener and I like my sense of humour.*

You can try that too. When you're sitting in silence, thinking about who you are, what are those traits you've identified in yourself? They might be good *and* bad. There are things that you might not like about yourself, but you can work on those things as well. It's about taking an honest look at yourself.

If what pops into your head is, 'I'm really funny and I'm so organised', feel good about those traits and say, 'Yes, this is who I am.' When you feel like you're aligned with who you are, you can feel it in your body. For example, if someone is creative and they're painting, they know they're aligned when they feel the energetic flow of being connected to their true self. My brother is a great example. He's recently started playing the guitar again. He's a creative, beautiful musician, but he hasn't played guitar for years because hasn't been in a position where he could just be himself.

It's important to stop and ask yourself: who are you when you're really aligned? Really listen to the answer. It's also important to *embrace that*.

For example, I might ask my best friend, Frenchy, 'How are you?' She runs her own company and her answer is often, 'I'm absolute boss vibes right now.

I just got another deal. I am loving it.' I think that attitude is amazing. And it should be celebrated.

It all begins with you

BY KRISTINE

Take a moment to think about what you **value and love** about yourself. When you do this exercise, try not to think about your appearance and what you see on the surface. Think of your inner qualities.

Some other questions you may like to ask yourself:

- What are your strengths?
- What challenges have you overcome?
- What do you value most about yourself?
- What makes you unique?
- What makes you smile?
- What inspires you?
- When do you feel happiest in your skin?
- What activity do you love to do that makes you forget about your phone?
- What words do you need to hear right now?

JOURNALLING

One practice that really helps me in the maintenance of my mental health is journalling. As I mentioned earlier, recently I've been doing it more regularly. I journal every night – well, I try to – and if I've had challenges throughout the day or if I've felt anxious or low, I try to figure out what triggered it and what I'm learning.

Journalling helps me to be a detective in my own life. If I'm feeling foggy or whatever it is, the temptation is to think that I'm feeling like that *right now* rather than wondering what led to that fog. Being able to go back through my journal entries helps me find out what got me to that point. Even if I don't get the answer, it's still a really useful exercise. For one thing, it makes me stop and just take a bit of time to look back rather than trying to rush on feeling the way I feel.

Psychologists talk about journalling, as do people who are preaching mindfulness. But it *is* so important. They say to journal every day, and sometimes that's not achievable, but even if you don't journal every day, it can help you work out when something changed. If you can't remember in your body or in your mind when you started feeling like you were going backwards or like you'd been derailed, you can look back and see, 'On Wednesday I was in a positive headspace. Somewhere between Wednesday and Friday something has caused me to take a turn.'

It's a really good step also to being self-aware and creating that awareness around what's happening in your mind and your body and your soul, and I think that awareness is the first step of healing.

If you're trying to work out how to bring this practice into your own life, here's how it works for me. I always have my journal next to my bed and when I'm having my morning coffee and I think of something, or I'm in the mindframe to do it, I'll journal. Before I go to bed, I'll always try to journal and sometimes I'll write pages and pages and pages and other times I'll do quick dot points of what happened in the day or what I'm grateful for – 'went for a walk, work was good, I'm okay'. It might only take a minute to list what I did that day or if there's anything to flag, good or bad.

I do think that people have this idea that journalling takes a lot of time but it doesn't have to and maybe the next day you'll feel like writing more. Some people just do little emojis or facial expressions of how they were feeling, or rank it out of ten, and these are really easy ways to keep track of how you're feeling and what's going on in your mind.

THINK ABOUT WHO YOU ARE AT YOUR CORE – WHO IS THAT PERSON AND WHAT DO YOU LIKE ABOUT THEM?

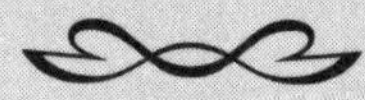

Change your language

I've shifted the way I see myself now and I tell my friends to do the same. I always say, 'Change the way you talk to yourself.' I pull my friends up on the way they talk to themselves. If they eat a meal and say something like, 'Oh, I'm a fat pig', I say, 'Change your language.' And they'll say, 'I really enjoyed my lunch.' 'That's better!' I'll say.

Of course I catch myself doing it, too. It's not like I've had some miraculous transformation. I still pick at myself, saying things like, 'I need to go to the gym. I'm bloated. I look tired and ugly.' Then I'll think, *Whoa whoa whoa whoa whoa.* I'll catch myself doing it and try to shift my thinking so instead it sounds like, 'I want to go to the gym so I feel healthier'. Because your choice of words actually affects the wiring in your brain. It changes the way you think when you change your language.

It's why affirmations are so great. I'd see people saying, 'Do positive affirmations.' And I would think, *What? This is so silly*. But I've found that affirmations do actually change your brain. They change the way you see yourself and your perspective. Every night in my journal I write, 'I am a goddess.' My psychologist told me to do that. She said, 'Look at yourself in the mirror and say, "I am a goddess." Say it every day, even when you don't believe it.' To be honest, I don't do it in the mirror but I do write it in my journal.

This simple affirmation has helped me change the way I see myself. I've seen the shift in my friends because they're doing it too. Anytime I feel like crap, they'll say, 'You're a goddess, don't forget', and I'll say, 'Yes! I am! Thank you for reminding me.'

As I mentioned earlier, I know there are some people who feel uncomfortable about other people liking themselves, and I think that comes from their own insecurities. They may be unhappy with some parts of themselves or feeling insecure. Anything that they push out onto you is just a reflection of them, and that's what you have to remind yourself.

There's also Tall Poppy Syndrome, particularly rife in Australia. You can see the culture trying to change to be more about sisterhood and supportive women, but sometimes it is a real challenge for people to feel comfortable about other people's success or happiness or milestone achievements. Some people just naturally see life as a competition. Being jealous and competitive is an ugly trait, I think. It disappoints me when I see people not supporting others – friends, colleagues or whoever – or being competitive with the person who's next to them. I wish these people would allow others to shine. Treating people in a positive way, building them up and celebrating their success ... it makes *you* feel good when you're supporting someone who's just landed a new job or bought a new house or whatever it is. If you're someone who finds another's success puts a spotlight on your own wins and losses, try to remember that this is *their* moment. Let them shine. It doesn't mean that you're not going to get there, it doesn't mean that they're better than you – it has nothing to do with you.

We're all on our own journeys. We all have different stories to tell. We're all here for different reasons. Ultimately we all have our own purpose in life, so our journey is going to be ours alone. You either have a choice to support other people's journeys or to feel jealous and insecure. Either way, you're going on your own path. So you can enjoy it, be happy, fulfilled and have beautiful friendships and a great support network, or you can be jealous and miserable and still on your own journey.

In my teens and early twenties I'd see beautiful women and think, *I don't look like that. Oh, she's prettier than me*. I'd feel so insecure. When I look back on these ugly parts of my personality that I didn't particularly like, I realise now – because I feel so free from it – that it's *tiring* thinking like that. Imagine constantly looking at someone else and thinking, *Wow, they're so shiny and beautiful*, and feeling miserable within yourself. That just sounds awful and exhausting and it's not how I want to live my life.

It takes work to recognise this pattern and make a change, but we can all choose our outlook on life. I choose positivity.

HOW YOU TALK TO YOURSELF
BY KRISTINE

If you think about it, the most important relationship we'll ever have is with ourselves. And how you talk to yourself is so important, because it's the soundtrack to your everyday life. The words you say to yourself, inside your own head, are never 'just words'. They are statements about how you want your life to go.

You've probably heard someone say that we would never talk to a friend the way we talk to ourselves – we would never say such hurtful things to a person we care about. Things like, 'I'm not good enough to deserve that job', 'I'm not pretty enough to have a boyfriend', 'If only I didn't look like this I'd be more successful or more popular'. Or even more harmful things like, 'You're so stupid – why did you do that?' and 'Don't be such an idiot', 'No one cares about you', 'No one's interested in anything you're doing'.

Why do we say such hurtful things to ourselves? Why do we think we deserve them? It seems to be easier to beat ourselves up than be kind, and we do it far too often.

Here are the reasons why I believe we struggle so much with self-acceptance and self-appreciation:

- We worry too much about what others may think.
- We worry about judgement from others and/or criticism or disapproval.
- We feel like we are 'behind'.
- We think we have too many setbacks.
- We don't think we are good enough.
- We have high expectations.
- We compare ourselves with others.
- We don't believe we are worthy – of love, happiness, success.
- We wish things were different.
- We often 'should' ourselves – *I should do this, I should do that.*
- We hold onto guilt and/or shame.
- We give our inner mean girl too much power.

Any one of these can stop us from showing up and from being the BEST version of ourselves.

But here's the good news: there is so much freedom when you can learn to let go of all expectations of yourself. Forgiveness plays a big part – and that means forgiving yourself, first and foremost.

In order to start on this path to freedom, I'm asking you to *stop talking to yourself in a negative way.* Just quit. Cold turkey.

You probably felt like laughing at that, right? Because, of course, it's easier said than done, and that's because negative self-talk is usually a habit and habits are hard to change.

Therefore, I'd like to give you a reason to stop talking negatively to yourself: *change your focus, as what you focus on will grow.* If you focus on bad things, they will grow in your life. And why would you want that to happen?

Start to look at yourself with love and kindness. Start appreciating yourself for everything that you are, right now – not what you think you should be or what you wish you were. Appreciate yourself right now, for who you are right now.

Self-appreciation is about turning the kindness you give to others inwards. And being grateful for yourself. What you see in others is simply a reflection of your own inner qualities.

Here's an activity to help you start:

- Take a moment now to jot down all the reasons why you are grateful for yourself.
- What do you value about yourself the most? Write that down too.
- Put that piece of paper next to your bed and look at it each morning or any time you're tempted to talk to yourself negatively.

Do you know the best time to start making this change? *Today.*

Start today. Start to look at yourself with love, with kindness.

Be grateful for yourself and all that you are.

Once you start to love, accept and appreciate yourself for all the wonderful qualities that you have, you'll begin to notice a flow-on effect in every aspect of your life. And it will impact everyone else around you, in a positive way!

DITCH THE MEAN GIRL
BY KRISTINE

Everyone has an inner critic. It is that voice inside your head that constantly feeds your negative chatter. In our workshops, we call that voice your 'Mean Girl'. Your mean girl (or mean boy) is all about expectations, labels, roles, judgement and so on. She lives in a state of fear and is constantly trying to keep you small. It's important to know that your mean girl is not your true self. She is not who you really are.

There is a real art in learning to quieten your inner mean girl and to not give her too much power. Here is a four-step method that I have learnt over the years that has helped me to silence my mean girl and to regain my power.

STEP 1 IS SELF-AWARENESS

When you notice that your inner critic is feeding you negative/self-hate chatter:

- Be present.
- Observe the thought.
- Notice the untruth.

For example: my mean girl always has negative things to say about my poor eyesight. She'll say things like: 'You look ugly wearing glasses' or 'You were born different to everyone else'. She'll even start saying things like, 'Why me?' or 'It's not fair'.

So in these moments, I stop.

I become present.

I become aware that my mean girl has shown up.

I am aware of the negative chatter and I notice the untruth. Because the *truth* is that I am beautiful no matter what. With or without glasses, my eyesight does not define who I am.

STEP 2 IS SELF-ACCEPTANCE

Lovingly accept yourself.

So instead of taking in the negative chatter, I stop and accept that, yes, I was born with poor eyesight. I don't buy into the 'You look ugly', 'Why me?', 'It's not fair', etc.

I simply lovingly accept that this is who I am.

Acceptance brings so much space as you no longer hold on to the baggage. You simply accept, as is.

STEP 3 IS GRATITUDE

Turn the negative chatter around and find joy. How fortunate that I was born with poor eyesight yet I still get to experience life. To see the beauty around me and watch my children grow.

If you can turn your negative chatter into gratitude, it's powerful stuff!

STEP 4 IS FORGIVENESS

Forgiveness allows you to let go and stop holding on. Forgiveness is a conscious decision to release all feelings of resentment.

So forgive yourself.

You can't change the past.

Let it go ...

Say it out loud if you need to, it can help you move on.

•

There is so much power in positive self-talk. Try the following to see how different they make you feel.

- Talk to yourself as you would a child: 'I know it's a little scary but I know you'll be okay.'

- Talk to yourself like your BFF: 'Nobody deserves this more than you! You are so fabulous!'
- Talk to yourself like your pet: 'We can stop for a little break, then we'll keep going!'
- Talk to yourself like your favourite indulgence: 'YES! You are 100 per cent worth it!'

And another thing: there is so much power in adding the word *yet.* If you can't do something right now, just add the word *yet. Yet* implies that something is achievable. *Yet* puts you back in charge and helps you grow and achieve your goals.

A really simple example of this is my eight-year-old daughter, who is currently learning to do cartwheels. I'll often hear her say, 'I can't do it!' and I'll say to her, 'You can't do it *yet.*' By simply adding the word 'yet', it gives hope and adds light at the end of your words. It instantly removes negativity.

My daughter will get there, I know she will. Practice makes progress. So the next time you say to yourself, 'I can't do it,' I invite you to add 'yet', and I have no doubt that you'll instantly notice a difference in your outlook.

HOW YOU TALK TO YOURSELF IS SO IMPORTANT, BECAUSE IT'S THE SOUNDTRACK TO YOUR EVERYDAY LIFE.

Stop that junk-food thinking

The truth is that saying mean things to yourself is junk-food thinking. In the moment it might feel good – it's an indulgence – but it's not good long term and it becomes a habit for too many of us. If you're thinking this way, like I was, it's the same thing as eating junk food regularly: you need to cut back and, ideally, cut it out.

Let's say you look at someone and think, *She's so much prettier than me* – I do this. But I'll try to catch myself having that thought and identify it: *Oh, that's a little bit of jealousy*, or, *That's a little bit of insecurity.* Labelling the feeling is really useful because it helps me recognise what's going on.

Then I follow that by saying to myself, *Well, that's not who* I *am. I know who I am at my core and I don't think that I'm a jealous person at all.*

When I catch myself having those junk-food thoughts, it's also an opportunity to wonder *why.* I'm not normally like that, so something has changed. Usually, junk-food thinking is a sign that I'm either tired or not feeling good about myself. Because when I'm feeling good about myself, and healthy and happy, I never even think about that sort of negative stuff. I never feel threatened or jealous or insecure about other women or like I'm not good enough.

My next step is to ask myself: *What can I do about that?* I think about what I need to do to somehow reconnect back to myself and feel centred. Sometimes I'll realise, *Okay, I'm feeling a bit overwhelmed and maybe I need to go and see my psych.* Or perhaps the answer is, *I'm tired and I need to sleep more*, or, *I haven't been to the gym for a week and I need to get some exercise.* Or I may just need to spend time with friends.

Trust me: there will be a reason why you're indulging in junk-food thinking and it will have nothing to do with the object of your thoughts. That pretty girl you're jealous of isn't the cause. Instead of feeling bad for having those thoughts, use them as an opportunity to figure out why you're having thoughts that are different to who you feel you are at your core. It doesn't take a special skill to do this. It's just a new habit you need to make.

The comparison trap

BY KRISTINE

There is no denying that comparing yourself to others destroys your own happiness. It's the thief of joy.

Some reminders:

- Be grateful. When you are grateful for what you have, you become less likely to be jealous of what others have.
- Remember, you only see the surface. Other people may have problems you don't know about.
- Find inspiration. Think a kind thought. Give the other person a compliment.
- Practise self-care.
- Tap into your own inner qualities and what makes you unique.

INSTEAD OF FEELING BAD FOR HAVING THOSE THOUGHTS, USE THEM AS AN OPPORTUNITY TO FIGURE OUT WHY YOU'RE HAVING THOUGHTS THAT ARE DIFFERENT TO WHO YOU FEEL YOU ARE AT YOUR CORE.

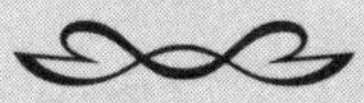

The social media vortex

Social media can be great. It helps you stay connected to your friends and family. You can see what your favourite musician or actor is up to, or find out about a new TV series. But I think we all know that it's not always good for our mental health.

You may have seen some attention given to a social media post I made. That post was a response to the vulnerability that so many people shared with me. Modern life can bring many stressors to the surface and living through this recent pandemic has magnified everything. So many of us are feeling broken and buffeted by anxiety and uncertainty – not just about our health but about jobs and what the future holds. I understood all that because I carry my own fear and confusion and I will never apologise for speaking about that. Sharing how we feel and what we are concerned about helps gather the knowledge and strength to overcome anxieties and to connect with others and learn.

I thank all those who kindly engaged with me at that time, who shared information and explained things to me that I hadn't considered. What that experience showed very clearly was the power of words – to draw us together or drive us apart. It gave me a greater understanding of the responsibilities a social platform demands. Dialogue is the key to understanding and this recent experience worried me because quick judgement and cruel words are never going to make a situation better. Kindness, an open mind and an open heart are the only ways any change can come, whether it be within society or within ourselves.

That being said, the social media experience isn't healthy for everyone.

Leaving aside trolling – and I can assure you I've had my fair share of that – just being on Instagram, for example, can mean you're constantly comparing yourself to other people, comparing your life to theirs, and sometimes feeling like you don't measure up. We have *all* been there.

Giving up social media entirely isn't always an option, though. Some people need it for work. Even if I wanted to deactivate or delete my personal Instagram profile, I'd still want to keep the profiles for BELIEVE and Stronger – by BELIEVE because they help me reach the people who need the information we have. So my work keeps me on social media. Facebook is less image-based but it can be a really hard environment to navigate when anyone can leave a comment on your posts. No matter how many times we say that it's 'just a photo' or 'just words', those photos and words can have a real-life impact on mental health. There have been so many stories – even one is too many – about teenagers, especially, suiciding after being trolled on social media, usually by people they know. That means social media doesn't just exist online; it has effects in the offline world too.

On top of the usual pressures of comparing yourself to other people online, when you're not feeling good about yourself and you're scrolling through, seeing people with these 'perfect' lives can be crushing.

I like to think that I'm not the type of person who compares my life to anybody else's, but during a recent Christmas holiday I was at home, and all my friends were away and my family were off doing their own things, so I was basically alone.

I was thinking, *Greeeat – I'm in my thirties by myself*, and I was looking at Instagram and all my friends were having these beautiful holidays with partners and kids, some are onto their second or third kid, and suddenly I'm sitting there wondering, *What am I doing with my life?* I never usually feel like that. I'm always really supportive of my friends going on their own life journeys with their families, and my friends are supportive of me taking my time and looking after me and my career.

After that I just became so low. Over that Christmas break I spent four days in bed. In a dark room. I was looking at my phone, at all these perfect bloody lives, and I felt so depressed. So behind. I couldn't take myself out of the Instagram world for long enough to say, 'You've got an amazing career, you have a beautiful home, you have dogs, you have amazing friends and family', because I was so sucked into the fact that I was by myself in a dark room at home while my friends were on holidays with their families. I really felt alone, physically and mentally.

On *Home and Away* we get a three-week break over Christmas and that whole three weeks I was down, I was out, and I ruined my time off because I was in this mindset of comparing my life to others. Social media was highlighting their beautiful lives, while I was thinking, *I don't have anything to post – I haven't done anything today. I'm literally lying here like a sloth and ... what? Am I going to take a photo of the dark room I'm in?* So I wasted that whole holiday.

I'm using this as an example of how badly you can get sucked in, even if you think you're self-aware about your social media usage. That was a situation when I got lost in it, and I didn't win that time.

When I'm feeling centred and present in my body, I can become aware that I'm starting to use my phone and social media too much. My eyes actually hurt – I don't know if anyone else's eyes hurt, but mine do. At that point I will stop myself and say, 'What are you doing, Sam?! *Get off it!*' As I'm sure we all know, it's too easy to lose hours on social media without even realising how much time has passed.

Unfortunately, social media has become a way for people to construct an identity that is not at all real but which has some benefits for them, and it can be so hard to work out what's real and what's not.

I don't even know if the people engaging in this sort of behaviour know they're doing it. It has just become habitual – probably because it's so easy to do.

There's no one-size-fits-all solution, but I have found that it helps to be mindful of your own social media usage, to see behaviours objectively, and to create distance from something happening to you and your reaction to it – in the gap between those is the space where you can try to see things logically. In the next chapter are some tips that have helped me take control of social media in my life.

I HAVE FOUND THAT IT HELPS TO BE MINDFUL OF YOUR OWN SOCIAL MEDIA USAGE, TO SEE BEHAVIOURS OBJECTIVELY, AND TO CREATE DISTANCE.

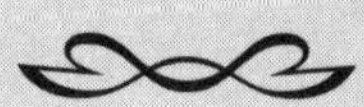

Taking control of social media

So here's the thing for those of you who can relate to my experiences but know you can't, or don't really want to, give up social media: you can limit the amount of time you spend on social media, without giving up on it entirely, and you will benefit from that. If it sounds hard to do, I understand, because I've been trying to do it too.

It's not easy for me to detox off my phone and off social media – but I have to do it for my mental health and my wellbeing. It's something that I have to consciously practise, too, so it's not something I'm expecting you to think happens with a click of your fingers. It involves you making a decision to reduce the role of social media in your life and then *making the decision again* every single day.

When I find myself scrolling for no reason, or I'm in a conversation and think, *Oh, I need to check this* or *I need to check that*, and I'm not being present in my life, that's when I know it's a problem. I really value my friendships and my connections with people and when I'm not being present with them because I'm thinking about my phone or social media, it's a red flag.

What I do with Instagram, for example, is delete the app. You can delete the app without deleting your account.

So whenever I catch myself spending too much time on Instagram, or if I see my friends with their happy families and I feel left behind or start comparing myself to them, or if I see a beautiful, fit woman and those destructive thoughts of *I'm not as pretty as her, I'm not as fit as her* come into my head ... I make myself delete the app. It's annoying to reload it, so anytime I'm tempted to use it again I often think, *Nah, it's annoying, I have to wait for it to load.* It makes me stop and think whether I *really* want to reload it or if I'm doing it because I think I should.

That doesn't mean it stays deleted but I often last a few days – and it's amazing how good I feel! I remember that the life I'm walking around in is actually real, not the vortex I go into when I'm on my phone. The connections I have to the real world are more important.

If you don't want to go to that extreme, though, there are simple things you can do like unfollowing the accounts that trigger you. If a certain person regularly makes you think you're not good enough, pretty enough, successful enough, or anytime a post makes you feel less-than, unfollow the account. If it's a friend who's annoying you but you don't want to create drama, mute their account. They won't know you've muted them.

These actions are all about trying to create healthy boundaries around your phone and social media. It's also important to create those boundaries around the things that *you* post. Be mindful of trying to show yourself authentically, and also be proud of what you post.

To be really honest, though, this whole social media culture is something that I'm still trying to navigate. I don't quite know what to do about it – how to balance the usefulness of it with the fact that it can be quite damaging. I'm figuring it out along the way. And to do that I basically just check in with myself when I feel unsure.

If any of this is resonating with you – and I think each and every one of us at some stage has had anxiety around social media – why not trying doing just one of the things I've suggested? My favourite tip: mute the account that triggers you the most. If there's someone you're following on Instagram who regularly makes you feel jealous because you think they have a better life/face/job than you, mute them right now. Or, if you don't know them personally, unfollow them.

Recently I went away to a mental health retreat and I spent two weeks without my phone. It was amazing to realise how anxious I felt about turning my phone on afterwards – because I'd been living in the real world and feeling really connected to myself. That moment really stuck with me.

Sometimes I get anxious when I go to reload the Instagram app and check it, and I think, *If I'm feeling anxious about reloading it, then just don't do it!*

I've even had to write down rules for myself to stay accountable about social media. For example, any time

I feel anxious or overwhelmed I have to turn off my phone and chuck it on the top of my wardrobe. I know that sounds drastic but to get it back I have to get a chair … and I'm lazy! So I'll toss my phone out of reach and I'll do something else to take my mind off it, like go for a walk.

I try to put the phone on top of the wardrobe as regularly as I can. Inevitably, what happens is that people say, 'I messaged you and it took you ages to reply.' My response? 'Sorry, I just needed a little digital detox.' They always understand.

What I've said about managing boundaries around social media also applies to text messages or any kind of direct messages. The ease of using our phones has meant that friends, colleagues, even strangers, expect 24/7 responses.

I've told my friends that I'm creating healthy boundaries around my phone because I'm trying to not be so anxious all the time. That means most of the time I don't have my phone with me unless I'm waiting for news or something like that. In this way I've made sure that I've managed their expectations around how regularly or quickly I'll communicate with them. So the people I care about don't get upset with me if I don't reply or don't like their photo or don't see their Instagram story – and, as I'm sure you know, people can get upset about that sort of stuff.

I tell my friends, 'I'll post my picture on social media and then I'll delete the app.' This means I don't sit there waiting for responses – *Do they like it? What are they saying about me?* Because that is yet *another* aspect of social media that can create anxiety: waiting for people to respond to what you've posted. Waiting for validation.

Expectations around response times also happen with email, and email can be just as anxiety-creating as social media. It was meant to make life easier for us, so we could communicate better and more quickly, and instead so many people feel like it's a burden.

I know a lot of people struggle with work email in particular. My friends have been talking about their work being able to contact them all the time through their emails. One of my girlfriends was getting so overwhelmed and stressed because her bosses were expecting replies from her at all hours. But she's not getting paid for 24-hours-a-day attention. I said to her, 'You need to tell your bosses that from a certain time in the evening, you're not accessible by email so you'll get back to them the next day. Then turn your damn phone off!'

That's just what I think she should do, but I don't have a boss who stresses me like that!

I had this same conversation with another friend recently and I said to him, 'Who said you're available 24/7?' He observed that I have boundaries when it comes to my energy and has said how much it's changed his perspective, spending time with me and seeing the way that I deal with things. When I need to work I give 110 per cent. I'm a good friend and I'm loyal and I'm always there for the people I love. But I'm not available 24/7. I allow myself to switch off from my emails, from my social media, from my phone, because I'm *living*. I'm in my home reading a book or spending time with my dogs. I don't feel the need to fill every second with noise, or let my seconds be filled with someone else's noise.

I think it's really important to set boundaries with your friends, too. My friends know that I'm a terrible replier. If it's urgent, of course I'll be there for them immediately. But I like to preserve my energy and my time and switch off my phone sometimes, because I'm not available to everyone 24/7 – I can't be if I want to look after my health.

If you're in a similar situation, think about what boundaries you might need to put in place around work emails during personal time, and also with your friends and family if you really feel like you need to limit the amount of time you're accessible.

Once I got an email from someone who had a notice under their signature saying what times they checked their email, which made it very clear that if you sent an email at other times it wouldn't be looked at straightaway. It may be hard to implement this with your work, but it's worth thinking about.

It wasn't *that* long ago that we didn't have to worry about our response times for anything. But now we need to say, 'Don't panic if I don't reply – I'm just living my life. I'm in the real world, not on my phone.' Maybe we should all start saying it, and actually doing it. Imagine if we all started living in the real world again?

I've finally made a bigger step towards that: I recently bought an old-school phone from the supermarket. It cost me 40 bucks, and all it does is call and text. No fancy camera or distracting apps. The only people who have that phone's number are work and my sister. In an ideal world I won't have my smartphone with me everywhere I go and I'll check it maybe once a day when I'm home; instead I'll carry around my old-school brick and just be present in the world and not have all that extra noise around me. I won't need to stress because I know work can contact me if they need to, and my sister can reach me for other important things. Once I'm in that groove I can just shut everything out.

Even before I bought the old-school handset, I've gone without a phone many times. I recommend it if you can, though nowadays it can be tricky. But trust me, my spiritual health will be in good shape with this new phone situation. Mentally I feel like it's going to be a game-changer, and I reckon more people should jump on that train.

Setting boundaries

BY KRISTINE

Setting boundaries is a form of self-care. When you set boundaries, you are putting yourself first and taking care of yourself. You are recognising what you need and asking for it.

Boundaries can help your overall wellbeing and create healthy relationships. Some examples are:

Saying 'no' to things because you're overtired – you are prioritising your need for rest.

Turning your phone off or putting it on 'do not disturb' – you are not available 24/7, you are protecting your energy.

If you don't set boundaries, you're likely to become resentful and exhausted. Without boundaries, you'll absorb other people's feelings and take responsibility for their problems. You'll allow others to take advantage of your kindness, and eventually this will negatively impact your overall wellbeing.

Tips on using social media

BY KRISTINE

While using social media and scrolling through your home page, I invite you to ask yourself, 'How does this make me feel?' It's a really important question, because social media should never make you feel not good enough or unworthy. Follow accounts that make you feel good. You are important. How you feel is important. So, if you ever get that icky 'I'm not good enough' feeling while scrolling past someone's fabulous, curated (and possibly fabricated) life, don't be afraid to block, delete, mute, or unfollow.

Remember that the majority of people only share their highlight reel, their glamorous side, the best version of themselves online. I read this quote once and I often share it with the teens that I work with: Being famous on Instagram is like being rich in Monopoly. It's not real life! Most people don't show their true self on social media. You only see a teeny-tiny snippet (which has probably been carefully selected from 20 versions of the same photo – gotta get 'that shot').

On the flip side to this, please know that once you post online, it will be on the internet forever (even if you delete it from your account).

Here are some questions that you may like to ask yourself before you post:

- Why am I posting this?
- Is it for likes?
- Is it to get attention?
- Is it for validation?
- For approval?
- To 'fit in'?
- Is this true to who I am?

My point here is to please be mindful when using social media. Keep true to you. And know that you are enough, just as you are. You don't have to shape or change who you are to 'fit in' or to be liked. You've got nothing to prove to anyone. The people you want in your life are those who love you for who you really are. At the end of the day, your happiness is much more important than the number of likes and followers. Be your true, authentic, wonderful self, always!

I LIKE TO PRESERVE MY ENERGY AND MY TIME AND SWITCH OFF MY PHONE SOMETIMES, BECAUSE **I'M NOT AVAILABLE TO EVERYONE 24/7** – I CAN'T BE IF I WANT TO LOOK AFTER MY HEALTH.

Self-sabotage

Whenever I'm in a relationship, the story I constantly tell myself is that *It's never going to work out for me* – and as you've already seen, this is something I recently realised I've been doing in many aspects of my life.

I would search for reasons why the relationship was not going to work out. I have reasons for this: I've been in an abusive relationship and a very toxic relationship, and I've dated the wrong people. Sometimes I wasn't the best version of myself, either.

But it didn't matter if I was in a really bad situation or a really good situation: this constant thought surrounding relationships is, *It's never going to work out for me.*

There was also a narrative that other people had created about me. They'd say, 'Oh Sam – she can never get it right, can she?' So there has been this line among people I know as well as in the media that I have not been able to find the right person for me.

I took on all of that judgement because I saw how people were seeing me. If another relationship didn't work out, then I'd think, *Dammit! They were right again*. There was a lot of shame and guilt – so much of it that I would try to make unhealthy relationships work because I was so scared of the judgement or that it wasn't going to work out, which meant that everything I was telling myself was true. So I hung onto things I shouldn't have – damaging relationships, toxic relationships – for much longer than I should have because I was so embarrassed that the relationship wasn't going to work out. It would be another failed relationship, and that would be a reflection on me. People would look at me with pity and say, 'She's so unlucky in love.'

The media certainly have not helped with that either. They'll write articles saying, 'These are all the men Sam dated!' And the worst part is that the articles are usually wrong: half of the men are usually friends, not boyfriends, and the other half are people I might have gone out with once or twice.

Of course, I do understand why there's media interest in my love life: I went on reality dating shows, so some people are invested in that area of my life. But the narrative of me having failed relationships began way before I 'won' *The Bachelor* and before people knew me.

This whole narrative has followed me for as long as I can remember – and it still does – but I feel like I'm more disconnected from it now because I'm trying not to listen to it or repeat it to myself.

It's something that I've been consciously working on over the past few months. I said to my psychologist, 'I carry so much shame for relationships that haven't worked out and so much embarrassment, and I feel humiliated that I've dated and it's failed, and now I'm where I am and it's still not working out for me.'

My psych replied, 'Oh, so you're telling me that you're a normal human when it comes to dating?'

I said, 'Well, it would work out for a couple of months or a week or maybe a year and then it wouldn't.'

'You're a normal human,' she said. 'Everyone dates and everyone has horror stories. Some also have wonderful stories. But everyone goes through this. The only difference is you're carrying so much damn shame about it.'

I still have to learn how to get rid of the shame surrounding my dating life. It's an ongoing process, because I don't think I'm over it yet, and I don't know the answer to solving it once and for all. I do know that I've had the narrative that *it's never going to work out* playing in my head over and over and over again so I stay in relationships I shouldn't, I look for reasons why it's not going to work out, I self-destruct, and I sabotage relationships before they've even begun.

If I meet a beautiful man who's kind and funny, I think, *Why are* you *going to love* me? *Of course you're not going to love me and I'll end up being hurt.* Or, *I'm going to ruin this and then you'll disappear.*

Even if I think I'm on the right track to overcoming this, I can still be standing in my own way. There was another brilliant psychologist I knew, and I said to her, 'Once I heal myself, then I'll find the right person,' and she said, 'No. That's not true. You don't just heal yourself. You're always going to have something to work on. You find someone who you grow with.'

These stories I've told myself – about how it's never going to work out for me and how I have to 'fix' myself before I find the right relationship – put a huge load on my shoulders. I was essentially taking on the responsibility of polishing the diamond to the nth degree to make sure that someone could see the sparkle. And that's exhausting!

I went through a stage in my early twenties when, for some reason, this whole idea of being 'marriage material' was a thing. I was so triggered by that because I thought, *What the hell does that mean? What is marriage material? I'm not a very good cook and I don't like cleaning.* Then I thought that being marriage material meant not having a playful side and not being silly. So then I would think, *In my next relationship I'm not going to be silly and playful.* I would try to hide that part of my personality.

To be honest, those parts of me are usually in full force and I don't think I could hide them if I tried. Now that I'm older I think, *Those are the* best *parts. Imagine marrying me – you're going to laugh your whole life. That seems like a real treat, you should be so lucky.*

So while I'm learning to deal with it, self-sabotage is something that's been quite big in my life. I know I'm not alone, because I've had messages from people who have done it to themselves as well. But we *all* need to stop getting in our own way. I've had to stop thinking that I need to 'fix' myself first, because that was another way I was self-sabotaging. It helps when I tell myself that I'm a goddess, and we need to find someone who treats us like that!

I SAID TO HER, 'ONCE I HEAL MYSELF, THEN I'LL FIND THE RIGHT PERSON,' AND SHE SAID, 'NO. THAT'S NOT TRUE. YOU DON'T JUST HEAL YOURSELF. YOU'RE ALWAYS GOING TO HAVE SOMETHING TO WORK ON. YOU FIND SOMEONE WHO YOU GROW WITH.'

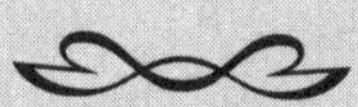

Grief

One of the hardest things – if not the hardest – we have to go through as human beings is grief. If I could make it so that no one would experience grief until they were old enough to handle it, I would, but it doesn't work that way. Grief finds us at all ages, and if we think we're ever ready for it, we're not. Usually it's grief for a person who has died but it can be for other things too: a friendship that has ended, a lost pet, a job redundancy. Death is usually the hardest to deal with but that doesn't mean that other forms of grief aren't as strong. It's important to acknowledge that, because you've probably encountered people who trivialise your grief by saying something 'isn't that bad'. If it feels bad to you, it *is* bad. It doesn't have to be a great catastrophe in someone else's eyes.

I wish grief didn't find me as early as it did. It is something that I have struggled with quite a lot in my life, and it's something I'm still affected by.

The biggest grief of my life so far came when I suddenly lost my beautiful stepdad Paul when I was 23. Paul raised me from when I was just a little girl. He was the most influential man in my life. He was such a stable parent and he loved me unconditionally. I was a pain in the arse and he just loved me anyway.

We lost him in 2012 to a stroke. On Sunday night he went to see the *Batman* movie with my brothers then the next day he had a headache and couldn't go to work. One of my brothers came home from school and found him on the ground. He'd had a stroke. He was only 55 years old and my younger brothers were in their teens.

When the doctors at the hospital explained he'd had a stroke and there was nothing else they could do for him, I remember I screamed. I screamed so loudly. '*What do you mean? What does that mean?*'

They repeated, 'There is nothing else we can do.'

I looked over to my little brothers and they were holding each other. I remember feeling like I was trapped. My body felt like it was on fire. My chest felt like it had caved in. Everything was just so surreal. It felt bizarre that this was even happening. I so desperately wanted the outcome to change.

Fortunately, Paul hung on and remained conscious for two days so we got to say our final goodbyes. I was there with my little brother Alex when Paul passed. It was the most difficult thing I've ever had to deal with in my whole life. I never thought I'd lose a parent suddenly and so young.

Afterwards, it felt like the whole world was spinning but I was standing still. I remember the frustration of thinking, *How are people even living their lives? How dare they?* The anger at how unfair it was. The injustice. That such a kind man could be taken away from us.

I think grief is one of those things where there's no rulebook. You never know how you're going to get through it.

You question your faith. You question everything, because this doesn't make sense. Seeing my family fall apart and seeing how broken everyone was – it's one of the darkest things I've ever experienced.

I know the feeling that there will never be light again. That I'm never going to smile again. I thought about all the things I was going to miss out on: I was never going to receive one of his hugs again, I was never going to feel his love physically. At the time I thought I would never feel his love again at all.

Paul would never see the boys finish school. He wouldn't be around when they got their driver's licences. He wouldn't be at my wedding. He would never be a grandparent.

That sadness takes a long, long time to shift.

Yet somehow, through the love of our family – my family is so strong, we've always had this deep connection to each other and fierce loyalty – we got through the initial loss. At first we just camped out in the lounge room together. There were doonas and pillows everywhere and all six of us kids were hanging out, talking, laughing, crying.

But in the aftermath of Paul's death, I struggled whenever I heard about someone dying or if someone had a stroke; even if they survived I'd be triggered and think, *The injustice that we lost him*. It's been something that I've had to work hard to get past.

For years after Paul's death I would get angry and scream, 'Where is he? If there is any afterlife, if there was anything, he would let me know he's here, and I haven't felt anything.' I desperately wanted a sign that he was still with us, a book to move from one side of the room to another, or some such thing. I desperately wanted hope. To feel connected to him, even though he was gone.

I suffered PTSD episodes – and it still affects me now. Recently, when I watched Patrick die on the TV show *Offspring* it triggered a huge PTSD episode. I still sometimes have hectic panic attacks – I can't breathe and my chest tightens. It's like I'm losing Paul all over again. I can vividly remember how it feels in my body to be grieving. In my chest, in my stomach. The pain is so raw and real, even though many years have passed. But it's as if it's happening again because we lost him so suddenly.

My mum and Paul had separated when I was 17. Then my mum met Pete, who was in our lives for 15 years. Pete was always a rock and his strength helped to hold us together. We, as a family, worked through the grief of losing Paul and my brothers losing their dad.

Recently I went to a mental health retreat for two weeks and while I was there I talked about the PTSD episodes I have and the grief of losing Paul. After I left the retreat, feeling enlightened, I learned that we were now going to lose Pete, who had been diagnosed with stage four lung cancer.

The news triggered me and I had a panic attack. I couldn't breathe, my chest tightened, I was screaming and crying. I was on the phone to Mum and to her credit she was an absolute saint. She just kept saying, 'Sam, you really need to breathe,' and talked me through the steps to calm down. Mum stayed on the phone with me until the panic attack passed.

Losing Paul was the worst thing I'd ever experienced, but the grief was compounded after Pete was diagnosed. What was different this time was that we were grieving every day for someone who was still with us. I'm grateful we had more time with Pete after his diagnosis, but it was just so hard knowing that our time would end.

Pete passed away while I was working on this book. I have lost two influential men in my life already and I can't quite believe it's happened. I'm still struggling with the unfairness, the injustice, the fact that our family has had to go through it again. All of this grief while we're still so young.

When I heard about Prince Philip dying, 'normal me' – in a stable frame of mind – would have felt empathy and sadness. But instead my grief made me feel angry rather than compassionate. I was thinking, *He lived to 99 but Paul and Pete died so much younger! It's just not fair!*

But sometimes life isn't fair. Death certainly isn't. That is what I'm learning.

The most difficult part of the grief of losing a loved one is knowing that, no matter what you do, nothing can change the outcome. It's such a hard thing to get through. It's something I'm trying to grapple with at the moment. I can't remember how I got through it last time, with Paul; it's something I am figuring out right now, with Pete.

This is not a part of the book where I tell you that I have answers from my own experience. What I have *is* my own experience, which I'm telling you about because it's so important that we share our stories. Grief doesn't end when you have a funeral. That is barely even the start of it.

Something else I want to talk about, because I don't think it's addressed enough, is that grief is a physical process as well as an emotional and psychological one. You really feel it in your body, and your body has to process it just as your mind has to.

I've always been a big believer in sitting in the pain and *feeling* it. I have seen my siblings who have not done that and the pain just manifests in different ways or will burst out of you unexpectedly later on. I feel what I need to feel – I feel sad when I need to feel sad. I think it is one of the hardest things to let yourself feel the grief. It makes you think about all the things you could have done better.

After Pete was diagnosed I said to my mum, 'You know how when we lose someone you go through all the different things you could have said or you could have done. "I could've visited his house that one time – why didn't I go?" Or "I should've said this" or "I could have done this and maybe things would have changed".'

When you lose someone you go into a tailspin about all the smarter choices you could have made to extend or make better use of your time together. It never ends.

Nine years after Paul died, I still have moments I reflect on: *Why did I do that? Why did I say this?* I beat myself up about it. I think about things I did as a teenager, when I was a real pain to my parents, and I think, *Why was I such a pain in the arse? You ungrateful little girl!*

Grief is just one of those things that you can't outrun. In grieving Pete this year, I've realised that you can have coping mechanisms to deal with it better but there are always going to be things that come up to trigger you, sometimes years later.

The other day my girlfriend asked, 'How are you?' and I said, 'I'm just tired.' When you're grieving that's probably the most common thing to feel. I feel tired. Tired of hanging on to hope. Tired of being strong. Tired of trying to figure it out. Tired of pretending everything's fine. I feel tired having conversations because I think, *None of this is important.* I hear people complaining about things and I think, *That's not important either.* I become dismissive of things that I deem irrelevant because *I've lost someone, I've got bigger shit going on than whatever you're worrying about – something so minor.* I know that normally I would never be so judgemental.

I look at people who have not experienced a similar hardship and 'normal me', who's not dealing with grief, would think, *Good for you.* But in the midst of grief – right now, in fact – I find it hard to connect with people who haven't dealt with the loss of a parent. I know it's because I'm grieving but I get frustrated with people who seem to have it easy – because I feel like my whole life I've been keeping strong and trying to create a beautiful life, and I keep getting hit after hit after hit. Right now it seems really unfair. It's hard. And I'm tired. It just doesn't seem to be getting any easier.

The truth about grief is, actually, it may not get easier. I don't know that we do become better with time. Maybe all we can do is get better at living our lives having grief as a companion.

Here's another truth: I don't know that we *should* get better at it. Grief is a part of loving people that we all have to deal with at some point. A decade down the track, it's okay to still be sad about someone who's died. There's nothing wrong with you if you feel that way. It means you loved that person so much that you continue to grieve and while I know from my own experience that grief can make living very hard, I don't think I want to stop grieving for these men I love.

Recently I was having a really bad night and I said to a friend, 'It's so unfair and I feel so sad, because the two men who raised me are just going to be photos on a wall and my children are never going to know them and they're probably going to be confused' – because my family may seem complicated from the outside but to us it makes perfect sense. 'It makes me angry that Pete and Paul are just going to have to be a story that I tell.'

He said to me, 'Well, I never met Paul but I feel like I know who he was, and I know that you don't need to worry about that sort of thing, because the way you carry yourself, and your values, and the stories that you share, he still lives on. So I know him because I know you.' He went on to remind me of a conversation we had when I was telling a story about my baby brother Josh and my friend said, 'He sounds exactly like his dad,' and I said, 'Yeah, he is.'

That made me feel so warm. I cried, a lot, when he said it, but it made me feel like I've done my job of keeping someone's memory alive, of keeping their spirit alive. The things I learnt from Paul will always be with me: to be kind to other people, to not be judgemental. I think that my family is the biggest priority in my life, and he was the one who taught me that family is family. 'Don't ever try to categorise our family,' he would say. We don't say the 'H word' in our house – half. We don't say half-brothers or half-sisters. People ask us, 'Is that your half-brother?' and we say, 'No, he's my brother.' They'll say, 'So who's ...' None of your business! Family is family and mine is united and we don't judge the make-up of other people's families. We have such a beautiful outlook on life and towards other people, and especially about family. All because of Paul.

If there is a benefit to the fact that I am still grieving for Paul nine years later – if I can offer you anything – it is that every single person in my life knows him. New friends know him and the role he played in my life. I share fun stories about him. I share hilarious things. I share his kindness and wisdom. His energy lives on. As does Pete's. I think about them both every single day.

Grief doesn't go away. You're going to have bad days on anniversaries or just because you're thinking of them. But I think the beauty in grief is that you see the values of the person you've lost and who they are live on through other people. I'm a believer that just because they're physically gone doesn't mean they're energetically or spiritually gone. Your beliefs about what happens after we die might be different, of course.

My two stepdads were completely different. Both of them had beautiful hearts, both of them had really strong family values. Paul was soft and compassionate and empathetic and such a beautiful, kind soul. Pete was a straight shooter. No bullshit. He was very direct and I love that. He made you laugh and laugh. They had opposite personalities but when I look at them as a whole it's like yin and yang. We all have a bit of both of them in us, and now I see them as our two angels.

GRIEF IS A PHYSICAL PROCESS AS WELL AS AN EMOTIONAL AND PSYCHOLOGICAL ONE. YOU REALLY FEEL IT IN YOUR BODY, AND YOUR BODY HAS TO PROCESS IT JUST AS YOUR MIND HAS TO.

Sometimes tomorrow isn't a better day

You probably know the phrase 'Everything happens for a reason'. It is used *a lot* these days. I use it often, myself. If you have something bad happen to you, one of your friends will likely try to make you feel better by telling you that 'Everything happens for a reason'.

Sometimes it can seem like that person is saying it to you because they really need to convince themselves of it. They might have had a bad time and they're determined to make the best of what's happened or determined to learn something from it so that they can manage better next time. Telling themselves 'Everything happens for a reason' is a way of doing that. That may be *your* reason for saying it, too.

With the same set of circumstances another person might have more of a victim mentality and think, *Why is this happening to me? It's like all these external forces are against me.*

I used to have a victim mentality in my late teens and early twenties. I couldn't believe the cards that were dealt to me. I've had my fair share of challenges, some of which I'm not ready to talk about. I thought everything was so unfair. And I tell you what, that wasn't working for me because I was drowning in depression. I was *drowning.* That's when I knew I needed to change the way I was looking at it.

I realised that had I not had those experiences I would not be the person I am today. I wouldn't be grateful for small things. I wouldn't be the woman I am. And I think that it is really important to try to find the lessons in hardship. To think, *Okay, that's happened – I'm going to make something of this, I'm going to learn something from this*, so that you are in charge and you're not letting 'the world' or 'the universe' or 'other people' be to blame.

It also helps to not build unrealistic expectations for yourself after something momentous happens. Hanging on to the phrase 'Everything happens for a reason' – as helpful as it can be – may mean you're then waiting for that reason to appear. What if it doesn't? How are you going to handle that? Or what if that reason does appear – are you going to recognise it? That one phrase puts a lot of expectation on a person who is already in a difficult spot to make something out of it. It can be really unhelpful for them. In fact, probably the only person it's helpful for is the person who said it – they feel better because they've offered 'support'.

I've got a group chat with a bunch of friends and recently one of them said, 'I'm just in shit, I've had a really bad day.'

I said, 'Look, I know today was a terrible day. And you know what? Tomorrow might be f***ed as well.'

One of the guys replied, 'What advice is that? That's the worst advice!'

I said, 'I'm just being realistic – tomorrow might be as bad as it was today. But you're going to be okay. I promise. You've got a great support network around you, and you're not alone.'

I was not going to say tomorrow is going to be a better day. Sometimes tomorrow isn't a better day.

Sometimes it's better to just acknowledge the fact that things are really bad and that there will be a point in time when it feels lighter and, instead of focusing on the bad now, it's more helpful to think, *Okay, well, this will be over soon.* But that always-look-on-the-bright-side-of-life kind of advice that's often given is not helpful to people who are feeling really, really awful.

To people who say, 'Oh, tomorrow is going to be a better day', I want to say, 'Maybe, but right now I feel so dark. I'm in the thick of it. And that comment doesn't help, instead I feel like no one understands.'

If you're trying to support someone who is having a tough time, a better way to say it is, 'Yeah, this is really hard and I'm sorry you're going through this. I'm with you every step of the way.' You can also say, 'You *are* going to get through this – I know it doesn't feel like that right now. But I'm right beside you. Tomorrow you might have another bad day, you might get another knock, but I'm right beside you.' That's the best advice I could give anyone who's supporting someone who is struggling. It's also important to remember that tomorrow *might* be a better day, after all. The day hasn't arrived yet. Don't put too many expectations on it.

Here's the thing: when you're working on moving away from that victim mentality, you might catch yourself slipping back into it. But just know this: it's all right to go back and forth between being the person who thinks tomorrow won't be a better day and the person who does. You can give yourself a break from the need to be positive all the time – the important thing is to recognise when you have a pattern of spiralling into negative thinking and realise that it takes constant maintenance work to not let that happen.

I know first-hand that when you get knocked down, that victim mentality might resurface again and you'll think, *This is so unfair – why is it happening to me?* There's nothing wrong with reacting like that. Some people who are struggling will have a day or two of their old patterns showing and they'll give up and say, 'See? I haven't changed.' I've been there too.

But when you think about it in the grand scheme of things, have you been having these episodes as often? No. Has it been as painful? Maybe. But is the duration as long? Probably not. It's important to acknowledge when your victim mentality doesn't last as long or happen as often, and that's a sign of growth.

I remember my psychologist saying to me, 'Sam, it's never going to go away completely. You are always going to have to put in the work, unfortunately. But when you go backwards you're still moving forwards. It's hard to go backwards but you are just growing and changing.' She's the one who told me it won't happen as often, won't be as painful and won't last as long.

So tomorrow may not be a better day, but you will learn something from your hardships, you're still moving forwards and you'll be okay.

Being the support person

BY KRISTINE

You may be reading this book not for yourself but because you're supporting someone who is experiencing mental health challenges, or you're trying to figure out how to help them – or perhaps you're at the stage of wondering if the person you care for is, in fact, having problems with their mental health.

Here are some signs to look out for in your loved one:

- withdrawal from others
- long-lasting sadness
- extremely high and low moods
- excessive fear, worry or anxiety
- dramatic changes in eating or sleeping habits.

The best way to start being of support is to reach out to that person and connect. Simply ask: *Are you okay?*

Then listen to what they have to say without judgement. Let them know you are there for them. Encourage them to seek help. Encourage them to get enough sleep, be physical and eat healthy food.

You may need to have this conversation more than once, and sometimes they'll need to be reassured that you really do care.

Being a support person to someone who may be struggling is an important role, but it can take a toll on you. Make sure you get support yourself – because you don't want to fall in a heap. There are sections on self-care in this book that can help you take care of yourself so you can better take care of others.

Looking after yourself as a support person is just as important as looking after the person in need.

IT IS REALLY IMPORTANT TO TRY TO FIND THE LESSONS IN HARDSHIP. TO THINK, OKAY, THAT'S HAPPENED — I'M GOING TO MAKE SOMETHING OF THIS, I'M GOING TO LEARN SOMETHING FROM THIS, SO THAT YOU ARE IN CHARGE.

Doing the work

I've mentioned before that maintaining my mental health takes work – regular maintenance work. It's something I do every day, because if I don't there are consequences. If you didn't brush your teeth every day, you'd end up needing a lot of dental work. While mental health maintenance can seem more difficult than brushing your teeth, it's the same principle: you'll end up with something more serious if you don't attend to it.

That doesn't mean that I don't resent the fact that I have to do this maintenance work. I go through stages. Sometimes I get really angry. I get angry at people who affected my mental health when I was much younger. I want to say to them, 'Do you understand that I now have to work on my mental health for the rest of my life?' And I get angry when my mental health affects my relationships.

It can feel really unfair if we have to go through this. An example: when I first read a definition of 'anxious attachment style in relationships', I recognised myself immediately. 'Insecure. Jealous.' Yep. 'Feeling like they're always going to leave you.' Yep. Reading all this made me feel hopeless – like I was never going to overcome this problem – but then I reminded myself of how far I'd already come.

If you don't know what your attachment style is, you can read up on them or take a simple quiz online. I've found that knowing my style is super useful in identifying triggers or things I want to work on.

These days I think I'm more secure. I'm not jealous anymore. Do I fear that people are going to leave me? Yeah, I still have that. But that's probably the only problem left. So, looking back at how I used to be I can see my growth, but when I was in it I couldn't. I still have moments in relationships where I feel like they're going to leave me and I have unnecessary anxiety and I think, *Oh, I'm still the same. I haven't changed.* But then when I step back and look at it, I'm not ticking as many negative boxes anymore. And that's how I measure growth.

When someone has really struggled with their mental health, as I have, I tend to see this maintenance work as acts of daily courage. You don't have to make grand gestures in order to make a big change, partly because you may slide backwards, then think you have to do the big gesture again to change. Maintenance work is you showing up every single day for yourself.

Every day you get up and commit these small acts of daily courage to address the past, to try to make yourself feel happy, whole and hardy for the future. You can just do these small things and they can aggregate to get you to the point where you're not ticking all those bad boxes anymore. If you are in a dark place, even making your bed in the morning is an act of courage, because it's taken you a lot of effort to actually get out of bed in the first place. Making that bed indicates that you are getting ready to face the day – and that's courageous too. If you've ever been in the situation where you're so depressed that you stay in bed all day, you'll know exactly how much courage it takes to make that bed.

I have a commitment to myself to always learn, grow and evolve. I'm sure there are always going to be things that I want to handle better and I'll never stop trying to be a better person. That doesn't mean that I don't like myself – I love myself. I'm gentler on myself now, too. I accept who I am. I accept myself for being anxious sometimes and having these triggers.

Do I still want to change? Yeah, I do. But I don't look at myself and think, *I'm so messed up.* Or, *I'm broken.* Instead I think, *Of course you feel like that. But you're working on it.* Even though there are parts of me that I still want to work on, I feel whole. I feel complete as a person and I wouldn't have been able to say that a couple of years ago.

You may think that committing to yourself to do this work, to deciding to actually *like* yourself, is an indulgence. Selfish, somehow. Here's how I look at it: it's an act of service to everyone around you to like who you are, because you're not putting the work of validating you onto them. It's actually the opposite of selfishness. It's saying, 'I'm taking responsibility for myself so that no one else has to do the work to make me feel better.'

I also think that when you do put in the work and you do like – and are more accepting of – who you are, you're a nicer friend, you're a more compassionate person, and you're better in relationships because you're more secure. You're more focused at your job. Everything benefits from you liking yourself.

Tips to calm the mind

BY KRISTINE

Sometimes when life can feel a little too much, you need to pause and literally take a few breaths. Here are some tips to help you calm the mind.

Slow and controlled breathing

The rhythm of the breath can help control the rhythm of the mind.

Exercise 1

Simply focusing on the count in this exercise can give your mind a rest when it's racing.

- Sit in a comfortable position with your eyes closed.

- Inhale for the count of 5.
- Pause.
- Exhale for the count of 5.
- Pause.
- Repeat for as many rounds as you need.

Exercise 2

- Sit in a comfortable position with your eyes closed.
- Become aware of your breathing. Breathing in. Breathing out.
- As you breathe in, say in your mind, 'Calm'.
- As you breathe out, say in your mind, 'Relax'.
- Repeat for as many rounds as you need.

Exercise 3

As you are breathing, repeat a calming phrase to yourself. Some examples are:

- 'I am safe.'
- 'I am loved.'
- 'This will pass.'
- 'I can handle this.'

Ground yourself

Grounding anchors you in the present, and into reality – taking the focus away from distress. Try one of the following:

- Splash your face with cold water.
- Carry a 'grounding' object – a small object that you can touch when you feel triggered.
- Check in with your five senses.
- Take a break. Take a walk outside and get some fresh air.
- Journal your thoughts.
- Reach out to someone you trust.

Affirmations

Here are some affirmations you can say to yourself when you're feeling overwhelmed or experiencing anxiety:

- 'This too shall pass.'
- 'I am stronger than I think.'
- 'I am in control.'
- 'I've survived this before and I'll survive it again.'
- 'My anxiety does not define me.'
- 'My feelings are allowed to be here.'
- 'I am enough.'

General tips

Try to focus on what you can control and let go of what you can't control.

My biggest tip would be to not look too far into the future, just take baby steps and take it a day at a time.

Breath by breath, step by step, day by day, you can and you will get through this.

Please know that you are not alone.

I LOVE MYSELF. I'M GENTLER ON MYSELF NOW, TOO. I ACCEPT WHO I AM. I ACCEPT MYSELF FOR BEING ANXIOUS SOMETIMES AND HAVING THESE TRIGGERS.

We all feel alone from time to time

I am really fortunate because I have five siblings I can rely on, always, the same way they can rely on me. I'm even luckier because I'm so close to my sister. Kristine is my rock and she's my go-to. I've also got beautiful friends who are like family to me, and I know I can call on them any time I need to.

However, even with all these loving people around me, sometimes I can still feel completely alone. And that's because I don't want to be a burden. Kristine has so much going on in her life – she's living in a different state to me, she's a mum and she's working, running all these workshops – and I think, *She doesn't need an extra cog in the machine to oil. I know that right now if I were to reach out to her she'd worry about me. It would cause her so much stress, especially since we're so far away from each other.*

So at times I have felt totally isolated because I didn't want to be a burden on other people, and it seemed easier to just not put my problems onto others and instead hide by myself. I know that this is a very, very common feeling in people who suffer with mental illness. And I know that some people don't have friends or family they can trust and that can feel really isolating, too.

But something I have learnt is that when I have kept a problem to myself and then told my sister I was really struggling *after* coming through the other side of the event, she would be so hurt and upset that I hadn't reached out to her while I was in the darkness. She would cry and say, 'You are never a burden. You're my sister. I'm upset that you didn't feel like you could reach out to me.'

So I think it's a really nice reminder for us that while sometimes you feel like you can't trust people or you don't want to burden them, people who love us want to help and it makes them feel connected. It strengthens our bonds. The best thing you can do when you are struggling is to reach out to someone – anyone.

Sometimes I've just been having a bad day and I'll share my problem with a colleague who I'm not particularly close with – it just comes out of my mouth – and from there we instantly form a connection. Because most of the time people have felt what you feel. They're just waiting for someone to acknowledge it.

Every time I have finally found the strength or courage to chat to someone and tell them what I've been struggling with, they've said, 'Yeah, I've felt like that before.' It's such a relief and the weight is lifted off your shoulders because you realise you're not alone. You realise that you can confide in other people despite your apprehension or your hesitation to reach out. It is the best thing you can ever do. You're reaching out and communicating with someone, and sharing the load does make it feel lighter.

I know you're possibly thinking, *I can't do that. I'm too scared to talk to someone in case they think I'm an idiot.* I completely understand that opening up like this is an act of bravery. It's not something I used to feel brave enough to do, either, so *I get it.*

But we are all connected to other people. We may feel like we're isolated, but there are billions of us on this planet together, all trying to make it through the day. You may not feel like you're connected to anyone else, but I bet you have had experiences where you meet someone and just feel a connection.

If that doesn't convince you, take a step back and realise that other people might feel the way you do. The person who sits next to you at work may really need to talk to someone and she or he is worried about how it will sound, even just to admit they're having a bad day. I come back to this idea of taking responsibility for your mental health: it's not always the other person's job to make the connection first. You can take that responsibility and I guarantee that you're more likely to have a good experience than not.

Part of taking that responsibility is seeking help. It is great if you tell a family member or friend how you are feeling, but most likely they are not qualified to give you all the help you need and, even if they were, it's better if you go to a third party for that. If you don't wish to tell your family member or friend everything that's going on, you could simply say to them that you need some help with your mental health and you'd really appreciate their assistance in finding a professional. Yes, it can be scary to admit even that, but you'll find that the act of taking responsibility by asking for help will make you feel stronger. Because you're *doing something.* Even if you don't want to tell anyone you know about what you're going through, I encourage you to do some research online to find out what's available to you.

Not everyone is able to see a psychologist, as I have been doing. But you may not know that your GP can organise a Mental Health Treatment Plan, which allows for several sessions with a psychologist that Medicare will cover. If you don't feel comfortable talking to your doctor, there are not-for-profit organisations like Lifeline that can help. Many workplaces have Employee Assistance Programs (EAPs) to provide counselling services, too.

Believe me when I say this: you may feel alone but you are really *not* alone in what you are going through. There are many wonderful people in this world who want to help you.

EVERY TIME I HAVE FINALLY FOUND THE STRENGTH OR COURAGE TO CHAT TO SOMEONE AND TELL THEM WHAT I'VE BEEN STRUGGLING WITH, THEY'VE SAID, 'YEAH, I'VE FELT LIKE THAT BEFORE.' IT'S SUCH A RELIEF AND THE WEIGHT IS LIFTED OFF YOUR SHOULDERS BECAUSE YOU REALISE YOU'RE NOT ALONE.

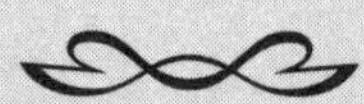

Body

You may be wondering why there's a section called 'Body' when my interest is in mental health, and that's because I know the two are absolutely linked. Not only in terms of how keeping yourself physically well can help keep you mentally well, but also in how your body can help you understand your state of mind.

What I've learnt is that our body always knows the truth and it always tries to teach us. But we don't listen sometimes.

When it comes to mental health, your body can also give you some clues. I've learnt that anytime I feel really exhausted I have to be very careful, because if I get triggered during my times of exhaustion I can go tumbling backwards, so I have to be mindful and look after myself.

Once you become aware of your body, you can feel when you're about to go into an unhealthy spiral. It's about becoming aware of those signs in your body then trying to implement the tools in your toolbelt to help you not fall as far back.

Because I get triggered by social media and my phone, I'll switch my phone off when I'm really exhausted. I limit my social media time. My friends notice that when I'm quieter on social media, generally I'm feeling tired or stressed and needing time out. When I'm active they know I'm in a better head space.

But there are other, very serious ways in which your body reflects the state of your mind and also the way you see yourself.

As well as providing some wonderful information throughout this part of the book, my sister, Kristine, has written one of the chapters. It's about body consciousness. Later in this section she also talks about self-care and I really encourage you to take her advice into your life.

Body image and self-consciousness

BY KRISTINE

Body image is something most teenage girls and women are conscious of and usually we struggle with it too. We are our own worst critics about how our bodies look and prioritising that over how we *feel* in our bodies.

When it comes to positive body image, I'm definitely no expert but what I do know is this: we are not born hating or disliking our bodies – it is something we learn over time. This means, therefore, it is something we can unlearn. I'm still working on this myself and I know I've got a long way to go. But I am so much more mindful of my thoughts and behaviours these days than I was 10-20 years ago.

In my late teens and twenties I was very body conscious. It started when I was around 14 or 15 years of age, when my body started developing. I got a bit curvier. I definitely noticed my mindset shift in terms of how I felt about my body. I very much compared myself to my friends and they were developing a lot faster than me.

In my early twenties I was very conscious of calories and my weight. I would weigh myself every day, I was very conscious of the foods I ate and I would even count every calorie that went into my body. If I ever ate chocolate or put on some weight (and I'm talking a few grams), I was so hard on myself. I hated myself for it.

I would do anything to look 'skinny'. Back then (for me) it was all about looking 'skinny'. And, at the end of the day, do you think this made me happy? No, no, it did not. I was never, ever satisfied with the way I looked. I was born with curvy hips, which I am learning to embrace now but back then I hated them (and I know that hate is a very harsh word, but that's how I truly felt).

My mindset about my body has only really shifted in the last couple of years. And still, to this day, I'm trying my best to navigate it because you can get trapped back in those thought patterns.

I met my husband when I was quite young – I was 15, he was 16. He was all about being natural and natural beauty. And at that time I would plaster my face with make-up, spend hours in the morning getting ready. He's helped me become the person I am today in terms of being more natural and not being so worried about these types of things, having curvier hips, not wearing make-up. I think too that I had very little self-belief and self-esteem so I felt extra pressure to look and be a certain way. It made me so self-conscious and stopped me from doing things that I might have enjoyed.

I was in Year 11 and I had enrolled in an outdoor education class. It was the beginning of the year and the teacher was telling us all the activities we would be doing throughout the year – we'd be going surfing, scuba diving, swimming, rock climbing, that type of thing. The moment I heard that we would be doing those activities I dropped out because I didn't want my peers to see me without make-up on and in my bathers.

I look back at that time and there's sadness there. If only I knew that it didn't really matter. But it stopped me from experiencing that class with my peers. I'm sure teens these days feel that way.

Where I picked up these behaviours and mentality, I can't quite tell you. All I know is that I just wanted to be 'perfect' and obviously I thought that meant being skinny.

I remember whenever I had a big event coming up – such as a friend's wedding – I'd say to myself, 'Okay, I've got six months to look skinny', or something along those lines. And when it came to my own wedding – gosh, look out! Things went to the next level. I went on a *very* strict diet so I would look 'my best' and 'skinny' on our special day. In the days leading up to the big day I hardly ate – it breaks my heart to think about this now, but at the time love and compassion for myself didn't even enter my mind.

It does, however, make for a very funny – and quite an embarrassing – story as at our reception I had a couple of alcoholic drinks and because I had hardly eaten ... It's fair to say I got a bit tipsy. I ended up leaving my own wedding with my dress over my head (I can't believe I just shared that!) and on the way home I was quite a sick little bride. Oh, my poor husband ... I've definitely learnt a lesson from that experience.

My point here is: it didn't have to be that way. I didn't have to go to that extreme level. I could have gone about things in a kinder, more loving and healthier way. And if you have thoughts about your body similar to the ones I used to have – you think you need to be 'skinny' or 'perfect' or just look different to the way you do now – I know that you could show yourself more love too.

There is, of course, no magic solution to these thoughts. But you can definitely unlearn them just as I have. We can absolutely train the brain to think differently. You need to be prepared for it to take time, though. At the end of this chapter you'll find some techniques to help you start.

Sam and I run workshops with teenage girls, through our organisation Stronger – by BELIEVE. In those workshops we talk to the teens firstly about acceptance – learning to accept that this is who you are and this how you look, to know that 'I'm enough just as I am' is a true statement, and also learning to embrace yourself. This doesn't apply only to teens, though – there are plenty of adults who need to accept themselves too.

These are some of the signs of poor body image, to watch out for in yourself or in others:

- Constantly thinking about your body and appearance.
- Comparing your body and appearance with other people.
- Changes to your eating and exercise behaviours.
- Weighing yourself frequently.
- Counting calories.
- Overcompensating at the gym for something you may have eaten or for having a day off exercise.
- Withdrawing from things you enjoy, like social activities or sports.

Accepting yourself is an act of self-care. It is to show kindness and compassion to yourself – the way you would to your friends – and to try to cut that inner critic we all have. Once we can accept that *yes, this is who I am*, it can bring a lot of freedom.

Whenever a crticial thought comes up I have to think about what that body part may do for me on a daily basis and try to steer it away from the appearance and the exterior. Because trying to look a certain way is exhausting and wastes a lot of time and energy (I talk more about this on page 166).

Really it's just learning to let go and say, 'You know what? This is me. This is who I am.' And learning to accept that and not try to be something or someone else.

Of course, it's easy to intend to do something. But I know all too well – and I'm sure you do also – that in changing our thinking about body image we have some challenges. The society we live in is a main – if not the only – reason we went from being children who had no negative thoughts about our bodies to people who really struggle to accept ourselves.

After the birth of both my girls I definitely felt pressure to lose my baby weight straightaway. This way of thinking was due to my own internal dialogue (the pressure I put on myself) but also, I felt external pressure from society.

When you see celebrities splashed all over the media just after they've given birth and they look amazing, you definitely feel the pressure to lose that weight when you've just carried a baby for nine months and given birth, and even though you aren't sleeping and you're just trying to get through.

When I see women who have just had babies and they talk about that pressure I always want to tell them to relax. It's so hard and so sad that we feel this way. Weight loss for appearance shouldn't be celebrated, and it certainly shouldn't be something that postnatal women should be concentrating on.

These pressures start so early. I'm so mindful of what my daughters are seeing and hearing in relation to this. One is four years old and the other one is eight.

Recently my four-year-old came up to me and said, 'Mama, do I look beautiful?' and immediately I thought, *Oh gosh, it's happening at four.* So I knelt down beside her and said, 'You know what's beautiful about you? You have a really beautiful heart inside.' But no matter I tell her I'm worried about what's coming for her, because girls can be quite competitive and often compare themselves to others. As much as I talk to teens about this, when it comes to my own girls it's difficult to navigate. I just hope that they don't feel the same way I did when I was growing up in terms of my worth being defined by my appearance. So far I feel like I'm doing a good job there but it's hard to say because they're still so young and girls are growing up so quickly these days.

The key to changing these thoughts and how we talk about ourselves and our bodies is, I believe, all to do with the language we use and also the way we compliment each other. The way that we compliment each other can be so appearance based. There needs to be some sort of shift in the way we talk to one another.

For me growing up it I was always told, 'Oh, you look so pretty'. It was all about my appearance. So obviously then I always felt the pressure to look 'pretty'. And it's the same for so many other people – we tend to give compliments based on appearance. Or if someone loses weight it's celebrated. So, what – before when you were a bit heavier you weren't as worthy as you are now?

When I was growing up, it felt like the way you looked defined your worth – and I don't think that's changed too much in terms of what teens are thinking.

In the workshops Sam and I run with teens, we play this compliment game. I always ask the girls to give each other compliments that aren't appearance based, because it makes them think, makes them think about the person's personality, what qualities they have, and we compliment each other that way.

They often struggle with it initially. And some girls still come up with, 'Oh, your hair looks so pretty'. We work together for numerous weeks, so they are familiar with each other, so then we just talk about the qualities that person has, and give them examples of how they could compliment each other, such as 'I'm so thankful I have you in my life.'

Even me, as an adult, I have to stop and think because I'll say things like, 'Oh wow, you look amazing!' So I understand how hard it can be to change those language habits. But it's worth trying – and persisting.

CHANGING YOUR LANGUAGE

I am all about affirmations. I think I started with them when I was a late teen and that's always helped me through.

Recently the Noosa Triathlon was on. I live on the Sunshine Coast and decided to enter a long time ago. Triathlons involve a swim leg, cycle leg and running leg.

Before the event I was feeling really nervous and anxious because swimming in the ocean is not my strength. A few days before I had a little panic attack in the ocean and I thought, *How will this go?*

I was off Noosa Main Beach and I was on my own. I panicked because I couldn't touch the bottom and I thought, *I can't do this*, and I had to swim in to the beach. I was so upset with myself. This was only a few days out from the triathlon and I said to my husband, 'I've lost my self-belief.' And he said, 'No, no, you know it's in there – you've just got to find it.' And I truly believe that with everybody. I believe that everyone has that self-belief. It's just sometimes hiding away and it's a matter of digging it out and knowing that you're capable. Because I know I'm capable of swimming that distance but I lost that self-belief in the days leading up.

I only learnt to swim three years ago. The moment I learnt to swim I registered to do a triathlon because I thought, *Now I can swim I can do this*. I think if

I can do it anyone can do it, definitely. It took a lot of early mornings, swimming at the pool. I've just started squad because I am determined to improve with my swimming. Once you make that decision and you change your mindset, anyone can achieve, I believe.

On the day of the triathlon I said to myself, 'Today I feel brave', and I just kept repeating that affirmation in my mind. This helped to boost my confidence and to feel mentally strong. I was prepared for anxiety to turn up in the ocean but this was important for me to overcome.

Just saying to myself, 'Today I feel brave', I was able to get through that swim and anxiety did not turn up and I do truly believe that it's because I kept repeating those affirmations to myself to get me through. Then when I got out of the water – whoa, I was so happy!

Sometimes you just have to stop and try to find that self-belief. For me that meant I had to find time for myself in the days leading up to the event, away from all the noise and distractions, to simply sit in stillness and breathe. Finding that quiet time is so important, it helps to settle the inner critic and bring you back home to yourself. I needed this time to remind myself that I was fully capable and could do it. And I did it! It took just over three hours. The swim was 1.5 km. It took me 39 minutes, which I feel is slow. And that's why I'm so determined to improve. But on the day it wasn't about the speed – it was about proving to myself that I could do it and overcome my anxiety. It was a good achievement for me.

When you're feeling disconnected from your body, moving it and testing it is a great way to reintegrate yourself into your body. Striving for something, like you do in a sport, can help you appreciate what your body can do. You can feel the improvements as you're pushing and challenging. There's a lot of emphasis on exercising to look good and not a lot on exercising the body just to be in your body and appreciate it for what it is.

Before I register for an event I always ask myself why – *Why am I going to do this?* I feel this is a really good question to ask because it sets up your foundation. I usually enter events to test myself (both mentally and physically) and I like having a goal to focus on. I also do it for my girls – to show them that you can achieve anything you put your mind to. They are my inspiration and motivation. Seeing their little faces when I cross the finish line makes it all worthwhile.

I did my first triathlon two years ago and once I finished it I thought, *Oh my gosh – I just did that!* There was self-discovery but also expansion because I thought, *What else can I do? Maybe I could go a little bit further or push myself in something else?* It proved to me that the body is so capable and so amazing, and it's not until you do these types of things and activities that you realise what it's fully capable of. Then you have so much more appreciation for it. You want to nourish it. You want to look after it. Because you only get one body.

Just as I ask myself what my intention is before I sign up for an event, I'd like you to try this the next time you think you need to change your appearance. Ask yourself 'Why?' – why is changing the way you look so important to you? – and if you're doing it to be happier. Initially, yes, you'll probably feel happier because it's something new and fresh but that's only short lived, over time it'll grow old. I believe happiness is an 'inner' job. External things aren't going to cut it.

POSITIVE BODY IMAGE

Having a positive body image isn't about having the 'perfect body'. It's about accepting and loving your body just the way it is – which can take some time to practise. Changing your body image starts with changing the way you think and feel about yourself.

It's only been in the last few years that I've changed my mentality. I now make decisions that are feeling based. And I always ask myself 'why'.

For example, I refuse to buy into the 'summer body' mentality. What even is that anyway? Why do we have to look 'hot' or have that 'summer bod'?

I refuse and extremely dislike 'before' and 'after' shots.

And I really dislike that weight loss is celebrated (just to make that point again!).

'In the end, we won't remember the most beautiful face and body. We will remember the most beautiful heart and soul.
– Unknown

Learning to embrace your appearance

Shift your focus away from your appearance and what you see on the surface, and start to focus on your actual body; what it **can** do and what it does for you each and every day without you even realising.

- Your lungs allow you to breathe in the fresh air.
- Your voice allows you to speak your truth.
- Your legs take you on adventures.
- Your eyes let you see all the beauty in the world.
- Your arms can hug your favourite people.
- Your taste buds allow you to taste delicious foods.
- Your nose allows you to smell beautiful scents.
- Your ears let you listen to your favourite music.

And I get that sometimes it's hard to shift your focus and I too sometimes get caught up in old thought patterns. But what I know for sure is this: **The way you look does not define your worth and it most definitely does not define who you are.**

I love this quote from an unknown source that I thought I'd share: **'Stop beating yourself up for everything you aren't and start loving yourself for everything you are!'**

ONCE WE CAN ACCEPT THAT YES, THIS IS WHO I AM, IT BRINGS A LOT OF FREEDOM.

The mind-body connection

Sometimes I feel like my mind is broken. Whenever that happens, my body feels a bit broken too.

I know that sensation in my body when things feel right. It always knows when a situation is right for you and when a person's right for you. It will know before you do. I reckon your body always knows first then your mind catches up.

It's the same when something is going wrong: your body will tell you. The problem a lot of us have is that we ignore what our body tells us because we think our brain – not our mind – knows better. Sometimes people don't trust their body and that's how they get themselves into pickles. We try to rationalise what's happening, telling ourselves our bodies are separate to our minds. Except they are really not. (If you're interested in learning more about this, I recommend the book *The Body Keeps the Score* by Bessel van der Kolk.)

For me, even if it doesn't consciously make sense, if my body says it feels right, I always listen to it now. But it hasn't always been the case: there have been so many times when I have decided to override what my body is telling me. That's how I know that now I have to trust it, because I've made so many mistakes. *So* many mistakes! My body says, 'Sammy, this isn't the right choice to make', and I'm like, 'Shut up! I'm going to do this.' A lot of the times it's about relationships and dating. My body says no, I have that feeling in the pit of my stomach, but I'm thinking, 'No, he's hot! Let me live!' Down the track I learn that person wasn't right for me and I know my body was trying to tell me this.

My advice to people is to sit in silence and listen to your intuition, because it always has the answers. You know in your gut that something's not right, when your body is telling you something, when you can't quite put your finger on why you don't trust someone or why this job isn't the right job for you – you can feel it. You hear people say all the time, 'I just can't put my finger on it.' Anytime someone says that, I say, 'I think that your body's trying to tell you something.' Obviously I don't know exactly what they're feeling but I think your gut instinct and your intuition always tells you what's going on. Sometimes I think it feels like a psychic ability.

I think the simplest example of trusting your gut is when you meet people and you know immediately if they're a good person, or if they're someone you instantly click with. Your body always tells you.

It works in positive ways and negative ways as well. I've had new people start at work and when I meet them I've felt their warm energy, their warm presence, and I've immediately connected with them and thought, *We're going to be friends.* That's a really beautiful example of it. Another example is when you meet someone and there's something in you that says, *I feel like I need to keep this person at arm's length* – because your body is telling you something's not quite right. And you might not be able to figure out what it is. Sometimes you just need to accept the fact that you don't know why.

In the past I have met people and felt like something wasn't quite right. But because I wanted to make friends I disregarded that feeling and continued to try to have a friendship with them. When it backfired and they broke my trust I said to myself, *I knew what my body was telling me but I didn't listen*.

Of course, wanting to be that person's friend came from a good place – maybe I was trying to be welcoming, or I really felt like I wanted to connect because perhaps they were a friend of a good friend of mine. But afterwards I always realise that I should have listened to what my body was telling me.

Listening to your body may not seem that straightforward, though, and it can take some practise – especially if you've spent years distrusting it or overriding it. Your energy levels can also play a part in whether you're able to listen to your body. When I'm really busy, when I'm stressed with work, I find it hard to listen to my body. I feel disconnected from my intuition and my spirituality and the core of myself when I'm distracted. The same applies if I haven't been sleeping well. And if I've been drinking alcohol on the weekend, for example – if I go out with my girlfriends, have a few wines, whatever – I always feel really out of balance. At those times I don't listen to my intuition. I can't even connect to it. It's there, though – never doubt that it is.

My psychologist once described it this way: throughout your life you've got this big computer that's processing every single thing on the subconscious level. So it's processing, processing, processing. You might feel a bit uncomfortable about something or someone makes you feel nervous or you're really anxious when you're about to go to work. Well, perhaps it's not the right job for you. Or there's something you need to change.

I certainly feel like that, even in ways that I sometimes can't describe. I remember when I was house-hunting – I knew that when I walked into the house that was meant to be my home, I would feel it. I walked through the door of the home I live in currently and I just knew. There was this overwhelming feeling that it was the right one. Now, my home – this home – is my sanctuary.

So now I try my best to always listen to my body because she talks for a reason.

On my screensaver and also on my wall at home I have an image containing these words: *Embrace the silence. That's where your power lies.* I really believe that. You hold all your power and your strength within yourself, and in the silence you can hear it speak. Listen closely, because it always gives you the answers.

TALKING ABOUT YOUR BODY WITH LOVE
BY KRISTINE

We all have something about our appearance that we don't love. Every single one of us has that 'thing'. For some people it may be that they don't like their nose, their ears, their legs, or their boobs. The list goes on and on. For me it's my thighs. I wish my thighs were thinner and more toned.

So when my 'thunder thighs' story comes up in my mind, I become aware of the thought (self-awareness), and I say to myself, 'Huh!? My thunder thighs story has come up.' Instead of buying into this story and getting trapped in my self-hate chatter, I dig deeper and go beyond the surface, and I think about what my legs do for me every single day. Where my legs have taken me.

What my legs have done and allowed me to experience. And what this does is it defuses the self-hating, negative chatter in my mind and turns it into gratitude and kindness. I'm so grateful for my legs as they have allowed me to complete half-marathons and triathlons, and they get me from A to B every single day.

Something we all need to remember is, our bodies are a sacred vessel and have been designed for experiencing life! There is no such thing as the 'perfect' body that we are striving for.

Think about all the time and energy you spend critiquing your appearance. Wishing you looked a certain way. That criticism and self-hate chatter wears you down, and it's so not worth it. Give yourself a break – that chatter is not worth your precious time.

Start giving yourself that love and compassion that you deserve. You are (we all are) so much more than what you see on the surface.

So, when you notice your inner critic/self-hate thoughts creeping in, instead of beating yourself up, give yourself some compassion. Say to yourself, 'It's okay', and gently guide your awareness back to the present moment, without any judgement or criticism.

Now, I have an activity for you. Grab yourself a bit of paper, and on the left-hand side of the page please write down all the things that you say you need. For example: whiter teeth, thinner thighs, fewer wrinkles, etc. Just write it all down.

Then on the right-hand side of the page, I'm going to tell you what you truly need. I invite you to write down this word: 'self-acceptance'.

Your body is amazing, **regardless** of how it looks! Your so-called 'flaws' are what make you unique. Learn to embrace them!

MY SELF-LOVE FORMULA

- Accept and embrace every unique facet that is you.
- Appreciate and value all that you are.
- Believe in yourself.
- Nurture your mind, body and soul.
- Love yourself. All love begins with you.

NOW I TRY MY BEST TO **ALWAYS LISTEN TO MY BODY** BECAUSE SHE TALKS FOR A REASON.

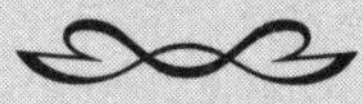

Taking care of things

As mentioned above, taking care of your body is an important part of taking care of your mind. We all know that we're meant to do a certain amount of exercise each day to keep ourselves in optimal health – but I'm actually not here to say you *must* do that every single day of your life. Because *I* don't.

There are times when I won't exercise. Right now, I haven't exercised for quite a while, especially during Sydney's 2021 lockdown. It was really hard to motivate myself to move, but I am also honest with myself about the fact that there are times when I'm more motivated to exercise than others. While I know that exercise is really important for overall wellbeing, I also know it's really important to not beat yourself up when you lose that motivation or you have a rest week or a rest two weeks.

I'm weather dependent as well – in winter I'm less motivated than I am in summer and my weight fluctuates. I just accept that that's life and I try not to stress about it, because I know that everyone is the same and it's unrealistic to maintain that constant motivation, constantly exercising and trying to reach that peak. So don't put too much pressure on yourself. Allow your motivation to fluctuate. Allow your weight to fluctuate, if that's what happens, and be okay with that.

However, if you've been having rest months – or years! – and what you're really looking for is some motivation to start exercising again, this is the advice I give to friends or to people who ask me about it: *set small goals*. Small goals help the reward system in your brain tick off items on that to-do list. Small goals make it easier to form a pattern and a habit. When I'm trying to get back into exercise after I've had a month or so off and I'm wanting to get motivated again, I'll just start small. I'll say to myself that twice a week I'll go for a walk around the block, or something manageable like that.

Why not try that yourself? Pick a manageable goal, like a walk around the block. It may take you ten minutes – great! That's ten more minutes of movement that you would have had otherwise. Once you're home again you can say to yourself, 'Oh, I did it. Tick!' There is so much gratification in ticking a box. Your brain loves that tick, tick, tick feeling (or you could write out a list and tick that, if you prefer). Then you realise how good you feel after achieving that goal, which snowballs into more motivation.

I think a lot of the time people feel guilty if they lose their momentum or they don't feel motivated. But what you're able to do really depends on what's going on around you.

Something else that is super important – and which can really affect your mental health – is sleep. I am not one of those people who falls into bed every night and has a great sleep. A lot of us aren't. But I *really* appreciate how important it is to try to have a good sleep, because if I have disrupted sleep, or if I'm not sleeping properly generally, I find that I'll feel quite overwhelmed, I'll be overthinking and feeling quite anxious – which means, naturally, that during the day

I'm not feeling at my prime, I'm not feeling focused, my head feels really cloudy and foggy.

It can be a chicken-and-egg situation too. In the times when I haven't been exercising and I've been eating more than I normally would have, my sleep has been affected – although having a bad night's sleep can also make it hard for me to feel motivated to take care of exercise and nutrition. But whichever came first – lack of sleep or lack of motivation – the result is that I feel like I'm hungover every day, and that fogginess absolutely affects my mental health. I find it difficult to connect with myself, so I end up not feeling centred and aligned. Plus I'm exhausted and moody.

In an ideal world I love going to bed by nine, reading for an hour, waking up feeling fresh, having had a good night's sleep. But sometimes that doesn't happen if lots of things are going on in my personal life or at work, and I'm feeling really overworked or exhausted, or there are lots of things on my mind. But then there's the flip side: sometimes I'm so unmotivated, I'm feeling so low, that I just sleep all day on the weekends.

If you also have trouble sleeping, there's something I do that often helps me, and may help you too: I move locations. If I'm really tossing and turning, I go to the couch and take my doona and pillow with me. I'll then almost immediately fall asleep. Sometimes I think the idea of still being in your own bed is the issue, because you've tried to fall asleep there and failed, and your mind can't let go of it. I'm sure I read a study somewhere that said when you change locations that actually helps because you associate your bed with not being able to sleep. But even if that study doesn't exist, I've told myself that it works.

The other morning, for example, I couldn't sleep. I woke up at three o'clock and went to the couch. I put on a kids TV show and fell asleep with my dogs on the couch. There's something quite childlike about that routine, but it's something that's really comforting for me.

Because sleep is so important to me, I have tried to create the right environment to facilitate a good night's sleep. My bedroom has no technology in it. I have no TV. I have nothing apart from blackout blinds, books everywhere, candles and plants.

Which brings me to another point: your environment. My room is something that I try to take good care of because when it is cluttered and messy, I find that I don't sleep properly. Generally the state of my house is a reflection of my mental health. If it's messy and cluttered, then usually my brain is messy and cluttered. But usually when it's clean, it's a reflection that I'm in a good mental health space.

Sometimes I'll look around at my home and see that it's cluttered and I realise that it's a sign that my mind is cluttered – and I hadn't realised it up until that time. For example, as I write this my house is a bomb. The whole week I've been so tired that I felt really foggy. I haven't been able to think properly. My mental health has been really up and down. I've been crying and having mood swings. And my house is absolutely a reflection of that.

Changing locations can work to help me sleep, and it can work for other things too. Sometimes when I know I really need to change my mindset or I'm just in need of a boost, I'm quite aware of the advice that's often given – to just 'go outside, go for a walk and get some fresh air'. But the idea of going outside, of putting runners on, can be too much. I do not want to do all of that.

So I'll just head out exactly the way I am – in my sloppy trackies or whatever – and I'll go for a drive. I think that helps. Especially when I feel so much pain and sadness, and I'm crying and feeling overwhelmed and trapped, the last thing I want to do is exercise. So I'll leave my phone at home and I'll go for a drive instead. Sometimes it's a long drive. Sometimes it's a short drive. But it just gets me out of the head space I was in. If you do it you may focus on driving or sometimes you may just still be crying – but either way you're getting out of the house, you're getting out of that loop. If you don't have a car you could catch a bus or a train or a ferry – whichever mode of public transport is nearby.

You may like to drive with music on but I drive in silence because it's a type of meditation for me. I can think clearly. I listen to music otherwise, especially when I'm cleaning and doing the boring things – I'll put on music and dance around the house and sing poorly while I'm doing it. But I know people think I'm strange because I do like silence quite a lot as well. Even when

I'm driving to work – for example, to Palm Beach in Sydney, where we film a lot of the exteriors for *Home and Away* – I usually drive in silence.

Sometimes I like listening to podcasts, but I just think driving is my time to be by myself and be alone with my thoughts, because every other time there's so much information – there are people calling, emailing, texting, and social media, TV shows to watch, work. There is always so much happening and so much stimulation that you need to just switch off. So I tend to use that driving time to switch off and be alone with my thoughts.

You may have read or heard a lot about mindfulness meditation, and I know meditation can be really useful, but I also think we can feel a lot of pressure to do it. Everyone's meditating, or saying they are. What I do know is that there's a form of meditation that will be right for you. For me, it's going for a drive. Or sometimes when I'm just drinking my coffee, instead of focusing on the actual practice of meditation, doing an activity like that in stillness is a form of meditation, as opposed to a more traditional practice like observing your breathing – although I do think that's important too.

The flip side of that is *too much stillness*. During lockdown with all its restrictions, people's mental health declined because the normal distractions that they used had been shut down. Going to the gym or seeing a friend – these are normal activities that we use to distract ourselves or to keep ourselves busy and occupied. They were taken away from us. So we were forced to sit alone in our thoughts for extended periods of time. Sometimes that can make you overthink everything; you can wind up feeling guilt about something you did three years ago. Certainly during lockdown I was thinking a lot about things that I'd pushed to the back of my brain and all the things I've done that feel shameful. Normally I'd just go to the gym or I'd see my friends and be distracted from those thoughts.

I guess the moral of the story is to find what works for you, with exercise, with sleep, with meditation. It will take trial and error – it certainly did for me. But I promise you that there's a balance that will work for you, and it's really worth finding out what that is because your quality of life will improve so much if you prioritise those three things.

SELF-CARE
BY KRISTINE

'Put yourself at the top of your to-do list every single day and the rest will fall into place.'
– Unknown

Self-care is what I'm *alllllll* about. It wasn't until I became a mum that I realised the importance of self-care. But you don't have to wait for that – you can start on self-care right now. It's about setting aside some time for yourself each day (guilt-free) and doing something that makes you feel happy and supports your physical, mental and emotional health. Or you could call it filling up your love tank or filling your cup – whichever term works!

It's so true what they say: you need to look after yourself first (fill your cup) before you can truly give to others.

So I'm here to remind you: YOU are important. YOU are number one. This is not a selfish thing to say. It's the truth.

Self-care is vital for your overall health and wellbeing.

When you've taken positive steps to care for your mind and body, your beautiful light shines through.

That doesn't mean that there's one set way to take care of yourself, because self-care can look different to everyone. It doesn't necessarily mean spending money, or taking a lot of time.

Self-care can be as simple as taking a little walk in your neighbourhood, making a cup of tea and getting some fresh air, listening to your favourite song or writing down three things you are grateful for.

If you're not sure how to incorporate self-care into your day, I'll show you how I do it in mine:

- I wake up before my children do, so I can exercise.
  I either go for a run, walk, practise yoga or do some strength training.
- I like to find ten minutes in my day for stillness.
  I usually do this after lunch when my four-year-old is sleeping and my older daughter is at school.
- I drink plenty of water, at least 2 to 3 litres a day.
- I like to burn essential oils. Lavender is my fave!
  I sometimes put a couple of drops on my pillow before I sleep too.

- I practise positive affirmations. The easiest way I do this is to write affirmations on my mirror in my bathroom, so every time I see one I read it to myself. The affirmation on my mirror at the moment says, *I am a true gift to the world.*
- I connect with family and friends often.
- And just before bed, I like to either read or journal.

SPARK JOY – EVERY DAY
BY KRISTINE

The phrase 'spark joy' was introduced to the world by Marie Kondo, and she was talking about objects in your house: when you're trying to declutter, only keep objects that spark joy.

But you don't have to save the idea of sparking joy for decluttering! Why not apply it to everything? Sure, there are some things we have to do in life that don't necessarily spark joy – folding washing comes to mind. We have other opportunities to find joy, though, and Sam and I certainly want to encourage you to find them.

The most efficient – and quick – way to introduce some joy into your life is to change something in your routine in order to shake things up. Try one – or more – of the following:

- Appreciate/practise gratitude.
- Make something (get creative).
- Learn a new skill.
- Connect with your people.
- Give a loved one a hug.
- Go outside.
- Observe your environment.
- Listen to music.
- Meet someone new.
- Go on an adventure (big or small).
- Reach out to an old friend.
- Volunteer.
- Play with an animal.
- Move in a way that makes you feel AMAZING! (Like dancing.)
- Pick or buy fresh flowers.
- Look up at the stars.
- Watch your favourite movie or TV series.
- Find something that makes you laugh.
- Watch the sunrise or sunset.
- Get some fresh air.

- Wear your favourite outfit.
- Have a bubble bath.
- Journal.
- Meditate.

SET SMALL GOALS. SMALL GOALS HELP THE REWARD SYSTEM IN YOUR BRAIN TICK OFF ITEMS ON THAT TO-DO LIST. SMALL GOALS MAKE IT EASIER TO FORM A PATTERN AND A HABIT.

Spirit

I wanted to include a section on spirit and spirituality because I believe this is so fundamental to our wellbeing. There are parts of our wellbeing we can clearly identify as 'mind' and some as 'body'. There are other parts that we can't define as clearly and they're probably 'spirit'. That's because, for me at least, spirituality encompasses it all. It's fundamental to who we are. To who I am. My *spirit* is me. That probably sounds a bit oodgie-boodgie but, hey, that's me.

What you'll find in this section are stories about how my spirit has been affected by various things that have happened and what I've done about that. Anything that has adversely affected my spirit has, in turn, affected my mental and physical health. Mind, body and spirit – they are intrinsically linked. We can't help one without attending to the others.

When other people let you down

Other people's behaviour towards us is something that, for me, is in the realm of spirit. As someone who has been in the public eye since 2014, I've met a lot of people who haven't behaved that nicely towards me, and there are still more people I've never actually met who also haven't been that nice. You could say it's part of the job, although these days, with social media, it's a little more intense than it used to be.

The first behavioural change I noticed way back in the *Bachelor* days was the difference in how people saw me – even friends I had then. I feel like, throughout my entire career, throughout my life, I've always been authentically myself. I've always been grounded. I don't think I've ever been caught up in the celebrity lifestyle or whatever people think it is. I feel like I'm just Sam from Lilydale, and I've always felt like that.

I entered the public world when I did *The Bachelor* – I don't even know what I was thinking in the first place! 25-year-old Sam thought, *This is a great idea.* And it was, in the end, because it led me to where I am now, for which I'm grateful. I learnt a lot about myself.

The *Bachelor* experience was a whirlwind but I do remember how it changed the way people in my life saw me – and these were people I'd known forever.

I remember a really wonderful girlfriend of mine, who was one of my best friends throughout high school, told me that she didn't want to be friends with me anymore. She said, 'I feel like our lives are going in two completely different directions and we're just on different paths and I don't want to be your friend.'

I was completely shocked. The show hadn't even aired yet and she had based her decision purely on the fact that I had taken part in it.

'This isn't who you are,' she said. 'Why would you go on a TV show?'

I tried to explain but I couldn't tell her what had happened – the post-finale outcome that everyone came to find out about. I was still processing it myself.

I said, 'I'm sorry you feel like that but it was a crazy experience and I really need my friends right now.'

'No, I think we're done,' was her reply.

That was heartbreaking – she was one of my best friends. I felt like I hadn't changed. I was the same person. I'd just gone and done this show, which was an interesting experience, but all I wanted afterwards was my friends and family who knew me, so I could feel safe again and feel like me again and process what had just happened.

She and I have reconnected now but it's never been the same. Losing that friendship was probably one of the hardest shifts for me. Part of why it was really difficult was because she had been through all my teens with me – she knew the struggles I'd had. Her family had been so good to me, they took me in when I needed it and made me feel safe and loved. So that friendship breakup was devastating and it happened purely because I'd chosen to do something that was outside of the box.

On top of that there were all these new people coming into my life wanting to be my friend. I made some mistakes with friendships. I like to think I see the best in everyone, I see the good in people, and I'm quite a vulnerable person, and those things can mean I'm naive sometimes – I was certainly a lot more naive back then. So I'd take friendships in, thinking that person genuinely wanted to be my friend. Then they'd sell stories about me to the media. There was one article in particular that hurt me deeply because it was such a betrayal of trust, but the good thing was that there was so much rubbish being written about me at the time that it sort of got washed away – but I knew that only certain people would know the details that ended up in the story about me, so I was pretty sure I knew who leaked it. I made plenty of mistakes trusting people when I didn't know them well enough.

I remember I was seeing this guy and I thought that he liked and respected me. Then I found out that he told all of his friends some very personal details about me, and about us, and bragged about it. I have never felt more exposed and disgusting. I was riddled with shame and guilt. Needless to say, that ended things between us pretty quickly.

Though it's led to some wonderful things in my life since, the months post-*Bachelor* were such an awful experience because some of the people I had loved and grown up with distanced themselves from me, and these new 'friends' were just selling stories. It was hard to date because people were using me. Grubby boys sharing stories about me. My trust in people was breached so many times.

Honestly, *The Bachelor* and what came after it was the most bizarre, unpredictable experience I've ever been through. Instead of supporting me, some of my friends were jealous because all this attention was on me. I guess the public started knowing who I was, so my profile was growing. And the people I wanted to be around the most felt uncomfortable about it. I don't know whether it was the Tall Poppy Syndrome I talked about earlier or something else, but I remember thinking, *I don't want it! I don't want it! Take this! Make it go away!* Because I just wanted to go back to what my life was like before this. I just wanted to be me again without this stuff attached, because I value good friendships and trust and privacy and it seemed like all of these things had just been blown up overnight.

I remember once I was checking into a hotel. It was really late, I'd flown in from somewhere for work, and it was this random place. This cute little old man at the desk – probably in his seventies – was checking me in and he said, 'Sam Frost? That's the same name as that girl in the news. Wouldn't you just feel so humiliated?' I'm thinking, *How does this old bloke know THAT*? My appearance had changed because I had blonde hair on *The Bachelor* but then I'd dyed my hair brown. He said, 'What do you think happened there?' and started brainstorming all these ideas. I felt like I was in *The Truman Show* or something. It was bizarre. I felt like saying, 'Just give me my damn key.'

It was so weird that people thought they knew me or knew what was happening in my life; that they were speculating about me. I was on a plane once and the people in front of me were talking about me. 'Yeah, yeah, he took off with this girl – it wasn't even the girl who was the runner-up, it was the third one. Oh god, how would you feel to be Sam?' This woman was yipping on the whole flight, telling her two seat-mates about the *Bachelor* stuff that was in the news. 'Oh, Sam got dumped' and blah blah blah. Once the plane landed she happened to turn around and I just looked at her and said, 'Hi.' She went pale. She was so embarrassed. I'm sure she learnt a lesson to keep your mouth shut because you never know who's behind you!

In a way, the *Bachelor* experience made me feel like there are several versions of myself out in the world. I hadn't fundamentally changed; it was just the details of my life that had. I felt like myself at my core but there were these versions of me that were starting to exist that other people were responding to – like the fakes who wanted to be my friends, and that close friend who decided she wanted no part of my life. These were really tough experiences for my mind to process.

I think a lot of how we feel about ourselves – even though we shouldn't, but we do – is due to how people perceive us. People's perception of who you are changes the way you feel because you can sense the judgement.

I always talk about my siblings, because we're really, really close; we're like a small army. They have never, ever changed the way they treat me, no matter what.

They've always supported me. They've been hesitant about things I want to do or they'll give their advice and say, 'Sammy, this isn't a good idea', or whatever. But, regardless, they'll help me, and they'll never stop supporting me and never stop loving me. They just see me for me. It's the most comforting thing, knowing that no matter what life throws at me, I always have that unwavering love and support. But I am very much aware that not everyone has even one person in their family they can rely on, and that breaks my heart. We all deserve to grow up with people who love us.

On top of the shifts in my established relationships, I moved from Melbourne to Sydney, and trying to make friends as an adult is hard. Especially if you've got a job that puts you in the public eye (people think they know you, or they want to be your friend for the wrong reasons).

I knew one person when I moved to Sydney – a beautiful friend, Sarah, and she was so generous. She would always say, 'Come to these places, come and meet my friends.' So I made friends by going outside my comfort zone. I'm actually quite introverted. I'm really comfortable with my group of friends, people who

I trust and love, but I can be quite shy, awkward and weird when I meet new people. I struggled for the first two years moving to Sydney; I felt really alone. I felt like an alien.

Making friends happened through trial and error, I guess. I was really fortunate that I did click with a couple of people and I think it came down to firstly having a wonderful friend to support me and hold my hand, quite literally. Sarah would say, 'You'll really like this person, you're quite similar in the way you see the world.'

I met my best friend, Frenchy, through a group of friends we were both hanging out with, although they weren't really my type of people. They were party people and I wasn't super into that. But then I met French. She was really funny and had similar interests to me. I instantly connected with her. From there we became friends, and then I made friends with her friends. My circle grew.

If you are trying to make friends in a new place, or from a new place in your life, I think the key thing is to not be afraid to go outside your comfort zone and to trust your intuition when you're doing it. If your body's telling you that someone isn't the right friend for you or a good person to hang out with, or if you're feeling like a situation you're in isn't where you want to be, trust that feeling and try not to force anything. You're allowed to leave an event!

I was in my mid-twenties when I came to Sydney. By that stage in life you know a lot more about yourself, so it's not like when you're a teen and you are shifting and morphing, trying to figure out who you are, and you meet new people easily because you're in new situations all the time. In your mid-twenties you pretty much know who you are, you know what you like. I think it's important to have a fairly strong sense of self when you are trying to form connections as an adult. It's also important to keep an open mind, even as you stay vigilant about your intuition.

I have friends who aren't necessarily the same kind of person as me. All my friends are random misfits; they're all weirdos and I love that because I'm a bit of a weirdo too. I connect with people who are authentically themselves, and I think other people appreciate that about me – I reckon we gravitate towards people who are true to themselves, true to their values. Sure, it's nice to meet like-minded people, but it's also great to have friends who have different opinions or see the world differently to you, because you have interesting conversations and they can broaden your mind a bit.

If you get nervous meeting people for the first time – that's normal! I just felt the nerves, went with them and tried to move past them. Anytime I would feel really anxious or self-conscious I'd tell myself that 'Everyone is usually thinking about themselves' – I don't say that as in self-centred, I mean that everyone is self-conscious, and they're usually not worrying about you. Even if it's not true, that's what I tell myself and it makes me feel less self-conscious.

It took me years to find friends who love me for me, and I'm so fortunate that I have these beautiful souls in my life. It's dwindled down to a select group of people now, and I did that by making mistakes. By being mistreated by so-called friends or people betraying my trust. My trust was betrayed a lot in friendship groups in the years after *The Bachelor.* But now I feel really loved and supported because I have a genuine friendship group.

I made some good friends when I was working on radio but certainly once I started on *Home and Away* and I had a foundation and a full-time job, that's when I was in the best position to make great friends. I feel like I have another family at *Home and Away*. And I have a group of friends there who see me clearly and love me for who I am at my core: a silly, weird dork with a sensitive soul. But it took me years to figure that out, to find true friends.

The kind of betrayal I experienced is shattering when it happens over and over again. But I haven't lost my faith in humanity, even though it would have been so easy to. That's because I think humans are generally good people. It goes back to my commitment to learning and evolving – anytime my trust was betrayed I'd think, *What did I learn?* I'd always go back to that. But what gets me into these hurtful positions *is* that faith. Because I believe in the good in people, I have made poor decisions with dating and with friendships.

Something else I've learnt, and I hope that this can help you if you find yourself in a situation where people hurt you, is that you can either sink or swim. Sometimes you're forced to swim – you have no other option. I don't know if I consciously make those decisions or it just happens that I have no other choice, because I go into survival mode. I think, *I'm not going to sink, I've got to move forwards.*

I do have to say that – because I have had relationships break down publicly – there's a lot of work that other people don't see. From the outside, because people can't see what's going on behind closed doors, they might say, 'Look how strong she is, she just keeps putting one foot in front of the other', when actually I do spend a great deal of time dealing with my problems privately before I ever tackle anything publicly.

Using the two relationships from *The Bachelor* and *The Bachelorette* as examples, what happened was that I went into my shell and dealt with the pain personally and privately: felt all the sadness, the humiliation and the embarrassment, the shame, all the things you feel when a relationship ends. On top of that I had to deal with the fact that these breakups were public and the media were speculating about the details and people I don't know are going to know about it all.

When things like that happen, I just deal with it internally. I'll spend time with my friends and my sister and the people I love, and I let myself feel whatever I need to feel. I grieve and cry and get to the bottom then I build myself up, and when I feel I'm in a place where I can tackle it publicly, that's when I'll mention it or I'll release a statement. I do that also because there was a stage in the media when every single thing they wrote about me was 'the jilted Bachelorette', 'unlucky-in-love Sam', and I wanted to change that narrative.

I'm not speaking on behalf of all women, but I've noticed it in myself, my friends and people who've reached out to me through social media, that some women do feel shame when a relationship breaks down, as if they're the failure. As if it's them and their weaknesses or that something must be wrong with them, or they believe that people think it must be their fault. And usually the dudes get off scot-free.

So I feel there is more pressure and expectation on women. We are conditioned to take responsibility for everything. So I really wanted to show women that we could change our own narrative. Particularly when the second relationship broke down, I didn't know what to say about it – it's hard enough to talk about something like that without being in the public eye. But I knew that people were watching.

I was very aware that there would be women who'd had their hearts broken witnessing my relationship breakdown and thinking, *How is she going to handle this?* I hoped my reaction would give them strength. I know personally I've seen people recover from marriage and relationship breakdowns and I think, *Gee, look at them go now! Look how strong they are. Look how fierce they are.* I look for and appreciate strength in other people, so I knew I had a responsibility to put one foot in front of the other and to be strong and get healthy. I also chose not to talk about it at all. Stayed silent. Kept my dignity.

Something tough to realise in the world of social media is that we don't always have to share our side of the story – we can just put one foot in front of the other and keep on going. Even in non-public relationship breakups! A friend of mine was talking to me about it the other day. He was worried that he'd look like the bad guy breaking up a relationship. People are so worried about what everyone else thinks when a relationship ends, and once you eliminate that and choose to look after yourself instead of trying to prove that you're the good guy in the relationship –

who cares? What matters is your health and your friendships and the supportive people around you, and making sure you feel strong and powerful and that your heart's healing.

I like to think that I'm a very authentic person and what you see is what you get, but I also do keep things private. There have been times when I've been asked questions, particularly when in relationships, to confirm or deny this or that, and answering honestly would make the other person look bad, but I didn't want that particular drama to be attached to me and my story. That's happened a couple of times. If something's happened to someone I know or someone I've dated and I've been asked a question to confirm or deny or elaborate, I think to myself, *Do I want this to be part of my story? No, I don't. I don't think they're worthy of being part of it.* So I've decided that it's better to keep some things to myself or to only share them with my closest friends. I guess it's all about managing your story and choosing what you want to be part of you. If it's some douchebag ex you're struggling to let go of: mate, cut the cord – you don't need that story attached to you. Leave them in the past where they belong.

IF YOU ARE TRYING TO MAKE FRIENDS IN A NEW PLACE, OR FROM A NEW PLACE IN YOUR LIFE, I THINK THE KEY THING IS TO NOT BE AFRAID TO GO OUTSIDE YOUR COMFORT ZONE AND TO TRUST YOUR INTUITION WHEN YOU'RE DOING IT.

Toxic relationships

Since I've introduced the subject of relationships, let's address the topic that features a lot in the messages I'm sent by people: toxic relationships.

I actually didn't realise I was in a toxic relationship until I started seeing a psychologist. I wasn't even in the relationship for very long but the shortness of time didn't lessen the impact. Looking back, I can see that there were many red flags in the beginning and I completely missed them because I was so caught up in the idea of finding 'the one'. I could not handle another failed relationship.

It comes back to what I've said about choosing your story. I didn't want another failed relationship to be part of mine. No way – not going to happen! Everyone is expecting this relationship to fail – I'm going to prove them wrong, regardless of what's happening on the inside.

There are so many parts of that relationship that still bother me. That still affect me. Because I was blind. Now I can see it happening to some of my girlfriends as well; I just want to stop them from making the same mistakes I did.

I think one of the most difficult things about being in a toxic relationship is that if they don't physically hurt or restrain you, it's hard to make yourself, or anyone else, believe it's abusive – because once someone makes physical contact, there's a clear line they've crossed. You say, 'That's abuse – that's not okay.' But with emotional, mental and psychological abuse, it happens more subtly, it happens sneakily. It's manipulation.

One of the first things that happened was that I realised he had isolated me from my friends. I'm such a social person and I love my friends and really value them. But he got into my head about the intentions my friends had and he would say things to me like, 'Are you sure they're your real friends? How come they're posting about you all the time on social media? Maybe they just want attention.' He would deliberately pick apart things about them.

At the beginning of the relationship he was very charming, very charismatic, saying, 'You're the most beautiful woman I've ever met. I want to marry you.' All the 'right' things. I was thinking, *Oh my goodness – no one has ever said this to me before. No one has ever wanted to marry me before. No one has ever said that I'm the one for them. This is amazing.*

That didn't last very long. A couple of months. But all during this time, while he was being charming, he was picking apart my friends. So then it very quickly became about me and him. That was the first sign I should have picked up on. The extreme charisma at the beginning, saying he wanted to marry me straightaway – it should have been a red flag. I'm not saying that if someone says that, they're a narcissist, because sometimes people do genuinely love you and know you're the one straightaway, but in my case it was a clue. There were other warnings too, like the first weekend I spent with him, he said, 'Can I have the passcode to your phone? Because I want to have a really open, trusting relationship. My ex was crazy. She was so insane.' He told me she was this, she was that, and I was thinking, *This woman must have been a monster!* So I said, 'Of course, here's my passcode. Let's create a trusting relationship.'

I would never go through anyone's phone so it didn't seem like a big deal to me. Now it seems bizarre that that was even asked of me, let alone on the first weekend I spent with him. But at the time I so desperately wanted to create a great, beautiful relationship with him that I said, 'Whatever you want, here it is.' Mind you, I didn't know his passcode; he just knew mine.

So it started with seemingly small things like that which I pushed aside, and over time I opened up about my upbringing. I told him about how my mum suffers from mental illness and how that's played a huge part in my life and how challenging that's been. I shared intimate details about my childhood, and all these things that I would never tell anyone else I shared with him. I was honest about my mental health and I even told him what my triggers were, like abandonment.

Meanwhile, he was collecting all this information about me in the guise of 'I love you, you're amazing and I want to know everything about you.'

Then everything started tumbling down. I started clueing on to his behaviour. I had women reaching out to me saying, 'Your boyfriend is sending me inappropriate messages', or 'Your boyfriend's asking me to come to his place on the weekend.' They would send me screenshots of messages he was sending them.

When I would confront him about it, he would use the information I had told him about my mental health struggles against me. He would say, 'I think you're paranoid. I think because of things that have happened in your past you're creating stories in your head.' I remember him saying, 'Why has every relationship of yours broken down? Why has it not worked? The common denominator is you, Sam. You are the problem.'

I had shared my insecurities about my failed relationships with him. Then he used it against me. So instead of answering the questions about why all these women were contacting me saying he's sleeping with them or sending them inappropriate messages, he twisted it around on to me.

He'd say things like, 'You have serious mental health issues.' Or, 'You're lucky I'm with you. No one else would put up with you. No one else would want this shit.' And, 'Maybe you're more like your mum than you think.'

I'd say, 'You're right, you're right. I'm sorry.' I'd cry and cry and cry.

All these things were so triggering for me. He knew that and would use them against me so I would be weak. Then when I was crying and screaming on the floor, feeling pathetic and broken and crazy, I'd think, *These girls are probably just making it up. They're probably lying*. Even though I had screenshots of his messages.

So I would be weak and broken and then he would comfort me. He'd say, 'It's okay, baby – I love you. Go and see a psychologist. You can get help.'

I'd think, *Oh, he does love me*, so I would stay in the relationship. It just went around and around and got worse and worse and worse.

One time I asked a completely innocent question – if the chocolate he was offering me was dark or milk – and he went off. He lost his temper and screamed and yelled and intimidated me. I said, 'No, no, no, I don't care which it is! I was just asking a question!' I panicked and cried. I soon became too scared to ask any questions.

He had so much control over me. Whenever I wanted to go and see my friends he'd say, 'Yeah, sure, that's fine – go and have a great time.' Then I'd go and he'd message me to say, 'You look like a slut.' He'd say that I was obviously going out to try to pick up, otherwise I wouldn't dress like that. He didn't want me to wear short skirts. He didn't want me to show my skin. He would always create a fight while I was out so then it would ruin my time. Yet he was going out, having the time of his life, and he wouldn't contact me. He'd completely disappear and I wouldn't speak to him all weekend.

These are only a few examples, but he did this sort of thing every day. Every day there was something he was picking at. Because he didn't want me to be strong. Any time I started feeling good about myself, he would put me down. He would knock me over.

I have never been so depressed in my life. I've never felt so weak. I lost all this weight because I was so anxious.

Meanwhile I was thinking about what I should do to keep his interest. I'd think, *Maybe I need to be sexier, maybe I need to be prettier. Maybe if I was prettier, he'd stay with me. Maybe if I could cook better dinners* – because I couldn't cook at the time and I thought that was a problem. *Maybe if I'm fitter. Maybe if I had bigger boobs.* I was doing everything I could to try to earn his love.

In short: I completely changed.

I remember one time he came over and I had just had my hair blow dried and I felt like I looked really pretty. I just wanted him to tell me I was beautiful. He completely looked past me and was complaining about his car.

I said, 'I made all this effort to look nice for you.'

He laughed and said, 'You're so pathetic.' I cried and he said, 'Now you're crying again. Do you know how pathetic you are? You seriously are a joke.'

Then he left and I didn't speak to him for a week. He would not answer any of my calls.

Whenever there was a problem, he'd say, 'Look at what you've done, Sam.' He'd convinced me that I was crazy because anytime I asked, 'Who are all these girls? Why are they saying all these things?' he'd say, 'You're crazy, something's wrong with you.'

So I ended up going to see a psychologist. I asked my sister to help me find a really good one because I just felt like I was so messed up. I thought, *I'm crazy. I have severe mental issues*. All these problems that I didn't have but his behaviour had led me to believe I did.

The first thing I said to the psychologist was, 'I need to fix myself because my relationship's falling apart, and I want to fix my relationship.'

As we were talking about the relationship and I was sharing this information, she was asking all these questions and I always had an excuse for him. 'Oh no, no, no, he does love me. He loves me. He loves me very much.'

After quite a few sessions, she told me that she thought I was in an abusive relationship. She said it very gently.

I responded, 'No, no, no, you've just got the wrong idea because I'm telling you all the bad things about the relationship.'

'I've seen this many times before,' she said, 'and I really feel like you're in an abusive relationship.'

She told me that she thought it was a good idea to create a space so I could distance myself from it and see it objectively. I don't really know exactly when I started seeing things clearly. I can't pinpoint a time. But I know when I ended up saying 'enough's enough'. I started seeing the psychologist in June and by October it was done.

It was after I started seeing the psychologist that he and I had a break that he imposed. He used to like giving me time limits. He'd say, 'I don't want to speak to you for the rest of the weekend', and he'd disappear. Or it was, 'I don't want to speak to you for a week.' And if I tried to contact him during that time he'd say, 'I told you that you're not allowed to contact me until the week is done.' He was trying to control me completely.

I was respectful of his time limits because I felt so weak around him and I'd try to do what he wanted. But if I needed to speak to him – something might've come up, like a friend's birthday party and I wanted to check if he was available on that date – I'd try to call him and realise my number was blocked. Then, after the weekend or week or whatever it was, he would unblock me and contact me because he wanted things to be 'normal' again. I thought it was bizarre, and of course it was really upsetting for me, but I just went along with it because I thought I was in love.

So after that episode he told me, 'I don't want to speak to you until the 24th of October.' I remember this specifically. I said, 'That's a month away.'

He said, 'I'm so busy with work, Sam, I don't need your shit. I don't need you asking me about girls. I don't need you crying all the time. I don't need to deal with you. You're too much. So you can talk to me on the 24th of October.'

'Wait – are we breaking up? What does this mean?' I asked.

'What part of the 24th of October don't you understand?' he said. Then he blocked my number.

I contacted him two weeks later on a different phone and he said, 'You are so pathetic, Sam. I've blocked your number. I don't want to talk to you until the 24th of October.'

'Are we in a relationship? Have we broken up?' I was so confused.

'I don't need to deal with you right now,' he said and hung up on me.

From that moment I thought, *Right. That's it.* And I went to stay with a friend.

I'd lost so much weight over the course of this relationship – I'd dropped to 47 kilograms. I'd just lost my job. I was so unwell. I was also furious at this stage.

So the 24th of October came and went. By then I'd blocked him on every single possible thing he could use to contact me. Then he called me from a different number, saying, 'I've been trying to contact you. When I said the 24th of October I wasn't breaking up with you, I was just stressed with work.'

I said, 'You know what? You can shove that date up your f***ing arse.'

He kept saying things like, 'I wasn't breaking up with you! That's not what I meant!'

And I said, 'Well, do you know what I'm doing right now? I'm breaking up with you. Never contact me again. You're abusive. You're a narcissist. I know that you've had plenty more victims than me.' I knew this because by this stage several of his exes had reached out to tell me about his abuse in their relationships.

'You're an abusive piece of shit,' I said. And that was the last time I ever spoke to him.

I want to be clear about what happened: it was slow-drip torture. At the time I was making excuses for his behaviour. I was the victim of this abusive relationship for the better part of a year. Every single part of my self-esteem had been picked apart. I was fragile.

I earnt more money than him and he hated it. He wanted me to quit my job. He wanted to have control over me – and he did have control over me. He was manipulative.

But on the outside it all looked wonderful. He would tell his friends, 'I love my girlfriend so much', which I knew because they'd tell me how wonderful he was. But he would say those things just so he could look like he was amazing. He had this image of himself of being a good guy – 'I love my family, I love my friends.' So everyone would say to me, 'Oh my goodness, you're so lucky!'

His fake presentation of our relationship helped me to start waking up and realising what I was in. I once had a wonderful, special thing happen and he was nasty to me about it, then he told his friends, 'She's so amazing. I'm so proud of her.' But that was so he looked like he was a supportive, amazing boyfriend when in fact he was quite the opposite.

So then I started seeing that he was obsessed with this image of himself, which was also, I think, a form of control.

Then I was getting gaslit, and not just by him. I would tell friends that he was behaving poorly and they'd say, 'But when I saw you last time he said how much he loves you – he seems like such a great guy.' I'd think, *Oh, does he? Maybe I've got it wrong* ... And that's how they get away with it.

There are things I'm still triggered by now. If I'm dating or in a relationship and someone needs space from me – like if we've had an argument and they say, 'I just need some space' – many people would say, 'Cool, no dramas, let's chat about it tomorrow.' Instead, I get severe anxiety, and this part of me is a wound that hasn't quite healed because he would just pull the pin on communication with me and I never knew when I was going to speak to him again.

Healing from this relationship has been an ongoing thing. I'm working on it, still, many, many years later. Fortunately, I'm learning to speak up so if I'm dating someone, I'll actually mention it: 'If you need time to do whatever you need to do, or we've had an argument and you need space, please tell me that you just need a moment and we'll check in the next day.' I need reassurance now that they're coming back to me because of the manipulation and abuse I experienced.

It's something that I have to consciously work on, which is hard. But I'm getting there.

What that person did to me was so cruel. It's one thing to be in a relationship with someone who is behaving badly but it's another when they weaponise you against yourself by collecting that information and then using it in the ways he did. They know exactly what they're doing. It's not this random insult flung at you in the heat of the moment. It's a very calculated way of using things you've said to hurt you.

I know now that someone like that is a predator and their sole mission is to destroy. It's really difficult to deal with it when you're not like that. That's why I felt like I was going crazy. Coming out the other side of it, my sense of self was very fragile, because he had done so much to dismantle it.

Trying to build myself up from that was a long journey. I feel like I'm in a good space now. But the healing process was kind of a beautiful thing as well, remembering who I was and all the things I wanted to do before this relationship sent things off-course.

I worked really closely with a psychologist all through this time, which changed my life, which is why I tell people to see a psychologist if they are able to.

Mine asked me once, 'Who were you before?'

I remember saying to her, 'I used to laugh. All the time. That's what I used to do. And I can't remember the last time I laughed. I used to be really silly, and I had this inner joy, this inner child who was so playful and fun, and I was such a free spirit. I can't remember what that feels like, to be that person, anymore.'

I felt so removed from who I was before. I get emotional remembering that time in my life because now I'm laughing all the time. I've found myself again.

When people who know me – especially if they've known me in recent times, rather than knowing me back then – think of me, they probably think about my laugh, about how much I laugh and how I always try to have fun. It's a huge part of who I am. And that was gone. Since then I have been figuring out who I am, and rediscovering the things that make me me.

That time does seem so foggy now. It feels like there was a cloud over my brain and my life for the time I was in that relationship, and more so healing from it.

There are so many things that are unanswered about what went on throughout that relationship. I've had to learn to let things go and accept that some things will never be answered. One thing I do know is that the problem wasn't me and I did nothing to deserve what happened.

I FEEL LIKE I'M IN A GOOD SPACE NOW. BUT THE HEALING PROCESS WAS KIND OF A BEAUTIFUL THING AS WELL, REMEMBERING WHO I WAS AND ALL THE THINGS I WANTED TO DO BEFORE THIS RELATIONSHIP SENT THINGS OFF-COURSE.

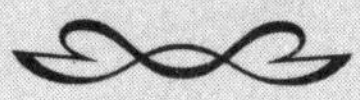

Gaslighting

One good thing about that toxic relationship, though: it made me aware of gaslighting. Nothing boils my blood like blatant gaslighting. You see it all the time. In workplaces, for example. If you're trying to hold someone accountable, if you get into trouble because someone's told you to do something and then their response is, 'I never said that', that's gaslighting. Then you start to doubt yourself: *Am I crazy? Did I make that up?* I know that feeling so well.

It happens at work, it happens in relationships, in friendships and it definitely happens on social media. Gaslighting is so damaging. It warps your perception of your life, of your reality. When you've been gaslit, you do wonder if something really happened, or if you made it up. It's used as a form of manipulation to either try to control you or to avoid accountability. But once you're educated enough on gaslighting, it's easy to recognise. I never hold back – don't you worry about that! – when someone's telling me about an experience they've had and I see it: I'll say, 'That's gaslighting. You're being gaslit.' Just to make it clear, though: while gaslighting involves lying, not all lies involve gaslighting. Gaslighting is what happens when someone sets out to make you think that you are crazy. They say up is down, and that they can't believe you ever thought up was up, and here are the reasons why up is down. That involves telling you lies, but it's done with a specific intent: to undermine your self-belief.

I will always flag gaslighting because I think it's important that people know what it looks like so that when it happens to them, they can look at it objectively and say, 'Okay, that person is gaslighting me.'

Sometimes I don't think it comes from a malicious place. Some people do it out of embarrassment or maybe they're struggling with their mental health. So you can't always say they're a bad person because they said they didn't do something when they did. There are exceptions. But they're a tiny minority.

But gaslighting is so triggering that you'll react emotionally most of the time, which makes it hard to see things logically and think, *Oh, that person's just trying to manipulate me.*

It can be very hard to combat a gaslighter when you're not one yourself, so the best you can do is try to protect yourself against it. When you realise that someone is telling you up is down and you *know* it's not – and trust me, you'll know – ask yourself why you would believe that person over what you know to be true. Is it because you want to believe them, perhaps because you love them and you don't want to believe that they could lie to you like that? If so, that doesn't mean you're a bad person – quite the opposite, because you want to believe the best in them. But believe the best in *yourself* before giving that to anyone else. Do not let anyone talk you out of what you know to be true, no matter how often they try. Trust your intuition and listen to your body, because I bet each time that person says something to you, you can feel in your body that something is wrong. Be aware that it can take time and practice to combat someone like this, but keep coming back to this important point: *believe in yourself first*. You may not succeed straightaway, but you will give yourself a fighting chance.

BELIEVE THE BEST IN YOURSELF BEFORE GIVING THAT TO ANYONE ELSE. DO NOT LET ANYONE TALK YOU OUT OF WHAT YOU KNOW TO BE TRUE, NO MATTER HOW OFTEN THEY TRY.

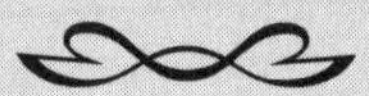

Bullying

My sister and I work with teenagers, we know that bullying is one of the biggest issues they're dealing with, and therefore one of the most important things we're trying to help them through. It's a huge problem. And bullying is not confined to what people say. We find that one of the main things people are dealing with related to bullying is exclusion – the bullies say to the target's friends things like, 'You can't talk to that person because that's someone we don't like, and if you want to be friends with me you shouldn't like them either.' This is a massive problem in schools at the moment.

I didn't really get bullied at school, and I know I was fortunate. But it has happened to me later in life.

I found that when I've been changing and growing, when I'm doing things outside the box and choosing new experiences or moving to different places, I've experienced bullying. With the rise of a career, I've found people changing the way they behave towards me, and I've felt that exclusion.

Mostly it's subtle, which is hard, because someone's not saying nasty things to my face. Instead, they're excluding me, turning people against me, gaslighting. It's like psychic attacks.

I've noticed – especially with other women – that if they see you as a threat, or when they're feeling insecure about themselves, they can project a lot of their insecurities onto you. That insecurity is the main reason for bullying, I think.

I've experienced this in the workplace before. I came into a new workplace where a colleague was similar to me in age, looks and personality type. I think she saw me as a threat, which I wasn't. (I can tell when someone starts sizing me up and I just want to say to them, 'Nah, you don't need to worry about me. You shine!')

When I notice that someone sees me as a threat, and they're excluding me by ignoring me in a room and talking to everyone else, avoiding eye contact, planning social events and inviting everyone except me, and I haven't done anything wrong apart from just existing, I wonder if it's because they're seeing something in me that they wish they were. Even if, in fact, they have nothing to be envious of! I tend to find that's what it is, because I'll analyse it and try to figure out why it's happening and why this person isn't warming to me.

I think naturally as humans we just want to connect to people and we want to be liked. People say, 'Not everyone's going to like you' – yeah, well, that hurts! I don't think that saying is super helpful. I get it, and they don't have to like me, but they don't have to be so hostile either.

Insecurity and the behaviour that results from it create a lot of tension in workplaces and schools. I think the core of the problem is that when people see a reflection of themselves, either good or bad, in you then that makes them want to exclude you.

What I do in that situation is deliberately shrink and be quieter. I will wear daggier clothes, I won't wear make-up. I will shrink myself so the message is, 'You shine. I'm not a threat.' I try to minimise their insecurities, I guess, or whatever's going on for them. 'I don't want your job. I don't want your boyfriend. I don't care. I just want to come in and do my job and have a nice experience.' If they're around I'll go quiet and I'll just do what I need to do, get in and get out.

I realise this means that I am managing someone else's insecurities in order to avoid being attacked, but I have discovered that it's preferable to the alternative.

I'm not sure what the solution for bullying is. There have been instances where I was the target and I reached out to the person and said, 'Hey, I don't know what's going on between us. It makes me feel uncomfortable, and I want to mend this relationship or figure out what this is because it's not a nice feeling being excluded.' That was actually received quite warmly and the behaviour has changed since. This person admitted that deep down she was actually quite fragile and sensitive. So once I understood that, I realised that the reason why this was happening was because of her own stuff. It's *always* their own stuff.

When we're working with teens about bullying, the one thing we emphasise is that 'it's not you – it's *them*, and they've got some issues or insecurities that they have to work through and that they may not even know exist, and they're just projecting all that onto you.' It applies to adults too.

You may think that having to minimise myself around a bully, being quieter, that sort of thing is an unreasonable response for me – or anyone – to have to do. And there *is* a mental health cost for me. But here's a possibly controversial thing to say: I always think it's worth it.

I would rather take the hit personally and internally than from the other person. I don't think that's the right answer – I don't think it's the right thing to do – but it helps *me*. I know that I need to get to a place where I can be myself fully and completely without dimming my light. Because if I had a daughter or if I think about my nieces, I would not want them to shrink themselves because someone's making them feel intimidated or threatening them or bullying them. That's the complete opposite of what I would want for them. But as an adult I find it hard to do otherwise. I would teach the lessons of 'just be strong' and 'keep being yourself' but actually doing that yourself can sometimes be a different story.

I want to say the right thing here – the most helpful thing. There's a lot of information out there saying that if you're being bullied, you need to be strong and just keep being yourself. But if *being yourself* is the reason you're being bullied, and knowing that you can't stop someone else bullying, trying to minimise the damage to yourself is the best solution I have come up with so far. Because 'be strong, don't change yourself' doesn't always work, and what it *can* do is make the target feel even worse if they're not strong all the time.

The coping strategy that works for me is one where I am not diminishing myself *to myself* and I'm not feeling less-than – I'm just making sure that my light isn't bright enough to attract that particular moth.

The secret to it working is that it doesn't bother me to do that because I quite like myself. I like who I am. Not wearing make-up doesn't bother me because I like what I look like. So it's easy for me to think, *I just won't make an effort in my appearance when you're around.* And here, unfortunately, it goes back to appearance again!

Or I'll be smaller. I'll keep more to myself. But I'm quite sensitive to energy as well. So when people have their big, confident personalities and their energies,

I sometimes get small. I withdraw a lot. I'll go and sit in my car – people probably think I'm so weird! I protect my energy. So I just keep to myself and do my own thing.

When I have to be around the person who is unkind to me, I try to build them up too. I'm always nice. I don't lower myself to their level. I don't ignore them. I don't exclude them. I invite them places. Anytime I'm in a group situation I'll invite them to join in. I extend my hand to say, 'I'm ready to connect when you are.' They don't usually accept, which is fine, but I'm letting them know that I'm still being true to myself. Because if I were to exclude them, if I were to not be kind, if I were to ignore them in the room – like they're treating me – that's just exhausting anyway and I can't be bothered living my life like that, and I think that's going to create more of a problem.

Coming to the place of liking myself first is the bedrock of the whole thing. I know that is hard to achieve because it's taken me a long time and a lot of work to get here. But once you are in that place and you know what your good qualities are and you are feeling confident within yourself, you can make these adjustments to minimise how bruising the world can be.

Part of what I hope this book can achieve is to help you get to a place where you like yourself as well. But there are also some little things you can do that can help you minimise the impact of other people's psychic attacks on you. Because when someone behaves like that, there is wear and tear on your energy levels. There are easy maintenance practices you can do to protect your energy.

Looking after my energy is essential when I feel particularly vulnerable, if the psychic attacks are coming strong at me all day and I can feel someone's envy, their jealousy, whatever it is – and that wears you down after you've spent a day with it or even a moment with it – I'll feel really overwhelmed, wondering, *What can I do?*

Sometimes what I will do is when I go to bed, I'll dim the room, light candles, light my incense. I'll lie down with my eyes closed and my palms up, and I'll breathe really slowly and deeply until I feel calm in my mind. Until I feel really clear and silent. Then I imagine putting a white light of energy around me and I visualise my bully and imagine them outside the white light bubble. So I protect my energy field and I say something to the effect of, 'I'm protecting my energy from this particular person and I'll fill up my energy aura with light and love.' Then I'll imagine this white glow around me.

I picture their venomous attacks – their exclusion, their words, their bullying – as green arrows and they're flinging them at me, but those arrows are bouncing off because I've got the white light bubble keeping me safe. This is a simple practice and it helps me feel clear and protected.

Dealing with bullying

BY KRISTINE

Bullying is more than just a fight or disliking someone. It's a misuse of power, with the intention to cause harm on purpose. It's really horrible.

Bullying behaviours can be verbal, physical, social and now, of course, there is cyberbullying, which is using technology to hurt someone.

Bullying is never okay. The effects it can have on the person on the receiving end can be detrimental.

Some tips if you are being bullied:

- Keep your distance from the bully.
- If it's online – you can restrict, block, report, delete or unfollow.
- Don't reciprocate or bully back.
- You can tell them what they are doing is not okay.
- And, if you are a young person, talk to an adult you trust and tell them what's going on.

A really important reminder for when someone is being unkind to you: their behaviour is actually a reflection of how they feel about themselves. So, the next time someone is rude to you at the shopping centre or when someone cuts you off while driving or when someone writes that nasty comment on social media, don't take it personally. Their behaviour has nothing to do with you. It's actually just a reflection of how they feel about themselves. Simply say to yourself, 'Gee, something must be going on for them right now', and leave it at that. Don't buy into it. Don't reciprocate. It's them, not you.

Be kind, always.

WORKING WITH TEENS
BY KRISTINE

Growing up I always knew that I wanted to work with children and teenagers but I just wasn't sure in which capacity.

Being a youth mentor has allowed me to facilitate supportive and nurturing workshops, courses, school programs and one-on-one mentoring sessions for pre-teen and teen girls across Australia and the world.

I became a youth mentor as I am so passionate about being a positive role model to the younger generation and to be that person who I needed most when I was growing up.

I take more of a 'big sister' approach with my mentoring. I'm another trusted adult in the teen's life who they can come to and someone who's not in their direct circle.

In that respect I consider myself as the bridge between the parent and the teen. I provide supportive and positive guidance. Sometimes I may not know the answers but I do know this: teens deserve to feel seen, to feel heard, to feel worthy and valued with no judgement.

WHAT I'VE LEARNT FROM MY TIME WORKING WITH TEENS

- Teens are very curious, brave and passionate.
- Teens feel emotions to the fullest.
- Problems teens are faced with can feel like the end of the world – which I totally get. I remember when I was a teen and if I had a falling out with a friend or a boyfriend, it felt like the end of the world. I wish I knew that this was a normal response back then.
- It is normal for teens to have a heightened sense of emotions.

MY ADVICE TO TEENS

- Be kind and gentle with yourself.
- Access support from an adult you trust and who can help take the load off.
- You're carrying a lot on your shoulders, but you don't have to go through this alone.

THE COPING STRATEGY THAT WORKS FOR ME IS ONE WHERE **I AM NOT DIMINISHING MYSELF** AND I'M NOT FEELING LESS-THAN – I'M JUST MAKING SURE THAT MY LIGHT ISN'T BRIGHT ENOUGH TO ATTRACT THAT PARTICULAR MOTH.

Acts of courage

When you're in a challenging place in your life, even getting out of bed in the morning can be an act of courage. But sometimes it's good to push yourself a little, because being courageous can help you build resilience.

Appearing on the TV special *The All New Monty* was a total act of courage for me. For one thing, it meant I had to learn a dance routine that ended with me taking my top off on stage in front of mostly strangers. *And* the whole process was being filmed to be shown to a TV audience.

Some of the things I do, I wonder, *What on earth was I thinking?* For someone who is an extremely anxious, paranoid, self-conscious person, I do some crazy stuff.

That whole journey of doing *The All New Monty* was a challenging experience. I feel like there was a huge shift in me.

I'd been to the previous live show and I was blown away by the participants' courage. Casey Donovan was up there and was an amazing powerhouse. Watching from the audience I thought, *Whoa – that must take so much strength and courage. How brave are they?* I just remember being so inspired by that and thinking, *I could never do that.* Sure enough the next season came and I was asked to be involved.

When I was first asked to do it, I said, 'I don't think so.' But then I spoke to Lynne McGranger, Rachael Finch and Georgie Parker, all these beautiful women who are great role models in my life and mentors and friends, and I asked them about their experience with the show.

They responded with things like, 'It was so liberating. I felt so empowered.' They talked about these breast cancer survivors who were in the audience, and where on the journey they met them. They shifted the focus from looking at our bodies in one way to objectively looking at them as these vessels that are full of miracles.

We can create life, we can fight cancer, we can heal wounds, we can rewire our brains, we can do triathlons. Our bodies are capable of so many miracles and they're incredible – we just need to look at them differently.

I remember having these conversations and thinking, *I have never thought of my body like that. I have always looked at it as what weight I am and how much food I'm eating.* So that's what got me over the edge and made me think, *Maybe I need to do this show. Maybe I need to do this for myself. Maybe I need to do this for other women.*

I'm always open to new opportunities. If people come to me with ideas, I'm usually quite open because I like challenging myself. Because you never grow in your comfort zone. You always grow when you're challenging yourself, when you're doing something outside the box. That's where your lessons come from. I admit I get bored if life is too easy. I don't want to live my life in the comfort zone. That sounds like a snoozefest.

If anything arises, especially when it comes to my job, relationships, whatever, if I have to make a decision, I always go into my room or somewhere I feel calm, light candles, breathe, find the stillness, feel centred, and then I'll ask the question. Because your intuition always knows the answer. When I asked myself about doing *The All New Monty* – when I was still and quiet – I knew I should do it. So I said yes.

We filmed the show over six weeks and at the beginning I was in my baggy-clothes mood and I didn't want to show any of my body.

I'm quite a vulnerable person and I wear my heart on my sleeve. I don't know how to be anything else. They asked me all sorts of questions on the show and if you watched it you would have seen how uncomfortable I was – I was anxious and paranoid and extremely self-conscious to the point where I just burst into tears, because all these beautiful women came in, they showed us how to do this dance and I thought, *What am I doing here?* I didn't think I would get through it.

On the show with me was Erin Holland, who's a beautiful model, and everyone else had dance experience, it seemed, and I didn't know to dance. I just felt so overwhelmed, and on top of that I had to take off my clothes, and I am not comfortable in my body.

Then I remembered why I was doing it. *For myself. For other women.* I kept saying it when I was on the show but it was so true – I kept being reminded of my purpose. We had these amazing women coming in and sharing their stories of surviving breast cancer, and they'd had their boobs removed and they'd lost all their hair. All the physical things that we're so focused on – our appearance and our body image – none of that matters in a circumstance like that because you go into survival mode. You've got to beat cancer. You've got to do it for your family and your sisters and your friends. It totally shifts the focus of how you see your body.

It was during that time that I realised that I wasn't really looking after my body, because all I was doing was starving it or feeding it, and I wasn't really exercising. During the filming of *Monty*, I really started to exercise – not because I wanted to look better, but because I wanted to look after my physical self in healthy ways. Throughout that six-week journey I really saw my body through a different lens and I think it changed the course of the next couple of years. I've definitely experienced a huge shift. I eat nourishing food, I exercise, I'm active, and I've certainly changed the way that I look at my body. I started realising what our bodies are actually capable of and truly appreciating that.

Women are phenomenal. I've always known that but I really *felt* it doing *Monty*, working with these women who were encouraging and supportive. That's why I always talk about the strength of the sisterhood. I always build my sister up; my friends too. It's so important to build other women up because the strength of the sisterhood can get you through anything, and I truly believe that.

By the time we were on the stage and stripping all our clothes off, I was having fun. The room was full of my friends, who thought I was a champion and so courageous. I wasn't even thinking about my body when I was up there on the day. I'd grown so far from that head space in the six weeks. The breast cancer survivors were in the audience, these beautiful women and their families, so being on stage was nothing compared to what they'd gone through. What we were doing was raising awareness for women to check their breasts and feel comfortable doing it. This was amazing!

I had the time of my life. It was such a fantastic and positive experience. Now I know why, when I asked Lynne, Rachael and Georgie if I should do the show, they said, 'Yes! It's so liberating!' It really was. I felt so strong and empowered. I felt like a boss queen. And I learned to appreciate my body for all it does for me, not just what it looks like.

PRACTISING GRATITUDE
BY KRISTINE

Gratitude is one of many positive emotions. It's about focusing on what's good in our lives and being thankful for the things we have. Gratitude is pausing to notice and appreciate the things that we may sometimes take for granted, like having a place to live, food, clean water, friends, family and so on.

It's taking a moment to reflect on how fortunate we are – whether it's a small thing or a big thing.

In positive psychology research, gratitude is strongly and consistently associated with greater happiness. Gratitude helps people feel more positive emotions, relish good experiences, improve their health, deal with adversity, and build strong relationships.

When we reflect on the good in our life, it tells our brains to take more notice of what's good. This helps pull our mind's focus away from what's bad, lacking or challenging. And that can make us generally happier.

Find ways to be grateful and embrace the simple things in your life. I promise you that it will change your outlook, and your life, for the better and it's so easy to do.

Some people find that writing down the things they're grateful for really helps them maintain the practice. You may find the following tips helpful.

Gratitude journal prompts

- A strength of mine for which I am grateful for is ...
- Something money can't buy that I am grateful for is ...
- Something that comforts me that I am grateful for is ...
- Something that's funny for which I am grateful is ...
- Something in nature that I am grateful for is ...
- A memory that I am grateful for is ...
- A challenge I am grateful for is ...
- Something beautiful that I am grateful for is ...

YOU ALWAYS GROW WHEN YOU'RE CHALLENGING YOURSELF, WHEN YOU'RE DOING SOMETHING **OUTSIDE THE BOX**. THAT'S WHERE YOUR LESSONS COME FROM.

Trusting your intuition

I never used to trust my intuition. That's how I made a lot of mistakes. But now I'm a huge believer in intuition and that's why mindfulness is so great, because it helps you tap into the intuitive part of yourself.

A lot of people reach out to me with their issues or problems, and I really like that they come to me because I feel that people know I'm not judgemental and I hold space for people, that I'm a good listener. I listen to everyone and what they're going through – all my beautiful friends, colleagues, whoever needs me – and my response is always the same: 'Well, what does your intuition tell you? It always knows the answer.'

But I've had to learn that the hard way. We often go against our gut instincts and when we do that we learn lessons. Then we say, 'I knew I shouldn't have done that. I don't know why I did it.' But we did it because we had a lesson to learn.

So I don't think that there's a wrong way or a right way. I think your life, and the flow of it, is easier if you listen to your intuition. But you're not always going to do that, and if you don't, it just means there's an important lesson you needed to learn so that's why you didn't listen. Even when you're in the thick of challenges – when you've made a mistake, you've done the wrong thing, you didn't listen to your intuition – you're growing and you're learning through it all. Had you not gone against your values or had you not gone against your intuition, you wouldn't have learnt these important lessons that will level you up to the next stage.

This relates to how I know when things aren't going so well for me.

I'll start with the place that I feel the most whole in myself – because that's how you know when something's wrong, when you don't feel aligned. So when I feel like I'm in the right place, when I'm in a really clear mindspace and I feel the healthiest mentally and physically, it's always when I feel aligned. I use that phrase a lot – when I'm talking to my friends or when I speak to my psychologist, I always talk about when I'm feeling aligned. Basically it's when I feel really grounded, when I feel really centred, when I can think clearly and I find it easy to meditate or to find the calm. When you can find the calm you can meditate, you can ask questions or things that you need guidance on. You have a strong intuition and it's easy to navigate through life.

That's the place I strive to be in most of the time. Because even when you have everyday stresses with work or relationships or friendships or family, the bumps don't affect you as much when you're coming from that place of feeling centred and aligned and healthy and happy. You may think, *That was stressful*, but it doesn't knock you down.

You always know something's not right when you're feeling foggy or low or unmotivated or fatigued. Generally they're the first signs for me of my mental health deteriorating. If I don't rest when I need to or if I don't look after myself during these times, my mental health will go backwards and I feel like I'll spiral. Before I know it I haven't exercised for two weeks, I've barely left my bed, I don't tidy around the house. It's so easy to fall into that trap. Then it's really hard, if you're feeling like that but you have no idea why. I think that's quite a common feeling, just talking to colleagues or friends. So many times I hear people say 'I just feel exhausted' or 'I feel flat and I don't know why'. I think that not knowing why can be really confusing and create a feeling of failure. Or being broken.

When I'm in that mindset and I know something's not right, what I try to do is retrace my steps. What has happened in the past couple of days or week that could have thrown me off centre? I try to work it out but sometimes you can't; sometimes life is just shit and for whatever reason you've just been derailed. This is why journalling can be helpful. It might not give you all the answers, but it may give you hints. Even if you can't work out why you're struggling, you shouldn't beat yourself up about it and think, *Oh great, I'm back here again. I take five steps forwards and ten steps backwards*. Instead, focus on finding your centre again.

In case you're wondering if feeling aligned with yourself is innate, I don't think I ever felt aligned when I was growing up. I always felt out of place, like I wasn't at home in myself – it's the weirdest feeling. I think it's only in the last two years that I've felt aligned, like I've found myself and I feel at home and at peace with myself.

That search to try to find my centre and my home within myself, it happened in different ways. I changed jobs, I moved around, I changed relationships. All that searching, really, was *Who am I? What do I want? What makes me happy and what makes me thrive and what brings me down?* It's learning and it's a lot of trial and error. Trying something and saying, *No, that doesn't feel right for my soul. No, that person's not good for me. This job makes me happy, this doesn't.* It's just figuring it out as you go. Some people experience this search especially during their teens and their twenties – they have this desperation to figure it all out. But I'm still figuring it out. At least I feel at home.

EVEN WHEN YOU'RE IN THE THICK OF CHALLENGES – WHEN YOU'VE MADE A MISTAKE, YOU'VE DONE THE WRONG THING, YOU DIDN'T LISTEN TO YOUR INTUITION – YOU'RE GROWING AND YOU'RE LEARNING THROUGH IT ALL.

Spirituality

At the end of my time at the mental health retreat I mentioned earlier, we all had to write notes about something we learned from other people or what we loved about them. Three of the notes talked about my spirituality. One of the ladies said, 'I love how connected you are to your spirituality.' Another one was talking about how I've taught them to open up and trust that everything's happening exactly how it's meant to.

I didn't realise how much of a role it actually played in my life until I saw it from the perspective of someone who just met me, particularly because all we talked about at the retreat was our mental health and obviously I hadn't realised how much my faith – or that relationship with my spirituality – really did go hand in hand with mental health.

I don't even know where to start with it. But the easiest way to describe the importance of spirituality is to talk about the way someone enters a room. We've all had that experience where some people enter a room and lift the energy up, while some people enter and bring it down.

I have really strong female friendships and a lot of the time they've started when I've met someone and I've instantly connected to them. That sense of 'I feel like we've known each other before, in another lifetime'. We hear those kinds of phrases all the time and they're probably the easiest way for people to learn basic things about their spiritual health.

Obviously there are so many different elements to it. But with someone's energy, you see them from afar and you see the way they light up a space or you're instantly drawn to them. I think that's all to do with spiritual health. It goes back to feeling centred and aligned. I think that's practising spirituality and practising mindfulness and getting clarity.

When you take a step back and think about your entire life, do you think about all the hiccups in the road? If I hadn't had that toxic relationship I wouldn't have gone to a psychologist, and if I hadn't gone to a psychologist I wouldn't have started my mental health platform, and if I hadn't started my mental health platform I wouldn't have found my light, my centre ... On it goes.

Every single thing that you thought was an awful period in your life – a relationship breakup, losing your job, being kicked out of your house, missing an opportunity – ends up redirecting you to where you're supposed to be and where you are right now.

Knowing that you will learn and grow from awful things that happen is so important when shit is going down, when you're in the thick of it and nothing is working out ... This happened to me when I was in a toxic relationship, I lost my job, I'd just bought a house and I didn't know how was I going to afford it. But the thing that got me through this terrible time was that I knew – I had this deep, intuitive knowing – that this was meant to happen for me and I just needed to go with it. I needed to feel whatever I felt. I needed to cry, be angry, whatever. Trusting that you're in the right spot and learning lessons doesn't mean you bottle it all up and don't feel anything. Absolutely feel everything.

Even if it hurts. Feel everything that you're supposed to feel. But know that this is what is supposed to be happening. In the bigger picture of your life, this pain has purpose.

Here's an example: I've spoken about losing my stepdad Paul and how it's one of the hardest experiences of my life and how unfair it felt that he was still so young when he died. When my sister was pregnant with her children, we often talked of our passed loved ones. Now I think about Paul and tell myself, *He's not going to let anything bad happen to those little girls, so don't worry about that.* I've always had this knowing that Paul's going to look after our family. Even with my career I genuinely feel like he has orchestrated this whole thing for me, to put me in a position where I can financially provide for our loved ones and look out for them. I'm extremely generous with my family because I feel like he trusts me to be. He's put me in this position because he trusts that I've got good intentions and that I'm going to put good out there and circle it back around to support my family.

I always imagine life as a river and you have all these obstacles but nonetheless you're going in the right direction, you're going in the flow of life, which includes hiccups and bumps. Sometimes we hang on so desperately to certain things we think are there to steady us in the water – even though you can feel life pulling you along. Quit your job. Leave the relationship. Signs are flashing at you left, right and centre, saying, 'Oi – wake up, wake up, wake up!' and you're hanging on, saying, 'No, no, no, I'm not going to listen – I'm just going to do this anyway.' You're trying to stop the flow of the river, you're trying to grab on to branches, you're trying to build blocks. You can hang on as long as you want but ultimately you have to go with the flow of the river anyway. So you can either make it easier or harder for yourself, depending on how connected you are and how closely you listen to your intuition.

Sometimes it's harder to practise that trust when you're in the thick of it. That's when you need to remember the bigger picture.

How did I get to this place of faith? It's kind of a weird story but ultimately it is why I am the way that I am.

It started when I was a kid and I was going through all these traumatic experiences with family stuff, and there were specific events that were pretty major in my life. I would be crying and crying and crying. I couldn't figure out why life had dealt me these cards because I felt like they were pretty shitty, to be honest, and I couldn't understand why bad things happen to good people. I was just a kid.

There were particular milestone events that were quite traumatic and after each one I'd be a mess. This next bit sounds ridiculous but this is genuinely what happened: the energy of a woman would come and visit me. She would hold me and tell me that everything was going to be okay. She told me things that were going to happen in my life. I always knew I was going to get the job on *Home and Away*, even though I wasn't an actor, even though I was just a kid. She would look me in the eye and say, 'You're going to have a beautiful life. You need to trust me – you're going to be okay and you're going to be able to support your family.' It would make me feel better and I'd have this sense of strength and power in me. Because I'd think, *What's happening right now isn't going to be my life. I'm going to be bigger than this. I'm going to have a great life – just you watch.*

The same woman would come and visit me at different ages – six, twelve, fifteen, eighteen – any time something terrible happened to me that left me in a mess. I never really understood what it was.

As an adult I'd forgotten that this had happened because I'd blocked out all those events in my young life, until I started seeing a psychologist. We were doing a mindfulness exercise one day and she said, 'I want you to go back in your life. I want you to feel deeply connected. Meditate. Sit in your body. Breathe.' She said, 'I want you to go back in your life and think about particular traumatic events that have happened, and what I want you to do is show up as who you are today and tell yourself you're going to be okay, you're going to have a wonderful life.'

I thought, *Oh my god, this has happened before*. I remembered the woman who would visit me when I was a kid. I bawled my eyes out. My head spun off. It was so bizarre.

But I knew what I had to do. I sat in my body and meditated. I felt really deeply connected to my higher self, my spirituality. I went back in time to those events and I told my younger self all these things. Even though

I'd already done it before. I don't know how to explain it. I don't *get* it. I don't even know how it's possible. But it happened. And I still get tingles every time I tell this story.

After I had that experience, though, I felt like everything was in its right place – a full-circle moment. But I know that there's still so much growth ahead of me. What I'm sure of is that I'm going to be a wonderfully wise old woman, even though right now there are still times when I feel like a mess. I'm still someone who can spiral. I still have days that I want to spend in bed. But I just know that one day this will all be part of my growth and part of my learning and I'm going to be able to pass on these experiences to help other people. It's strange to realise I might be doing that right now. Sometimes I think that I feel pain so that I can empathise. I remember thinking that quite recently – *Oh god, why am I feeling so much pain still? Why am I hurting so badly?* Then I get a feeling that I need to pass this knowledge on and it's just going to make me have a deeper ability to connect with other people.

ABSOLUTELY **FEEL EVERYTHING.**
EVEN IF IT HURTS. FEEL EVERYTHING
THAT YOU'RE SUPPOSED TO FEEL.
BUT KNOW THAT THIS IS WHAT IS
SUPPOSED TO BE HAPPENING.

A last word

So here we are. You know a lot more about me than you did at the start of this book – and I also hope you know a lot more about yourself. *Or* that you plan to find out a lot more about yourself.

I'm so grateful to the people who have supported me and cheered me along the way. All the people who have randomly messaged me or emailed me, or who have walked up to me in the street and said, 'Thank you so much for talking about mental health – it really helped me get through a bad time.'

So many people who have reached out to me will never know how much of a positive impact that has had on my life. There are days when I felt like I could not possibly get through the next day. I felt so dark and heavy, and like no one wanted me around. And I would receive a message or an email from someone out there that brightened my day.

I don't think people realise how much light they have and how much something small like a message just to say thank you can change someone's life. That's what people have done for me.

While editing this book I was going through turmoil. But I was reading my own words and thinking, *I should take my own advice* – which we sometimes forget to do. I realised how important some of the things I was saying were to me. I needed to read my own words and they helped me get through it. One day I was reading the part where I said if you don't feel like you can go outside because you can't even bring yourself to have a shower, go for a drive. That day I left my phone at home and went for a drive, three hours south and three hours back. During that time I came to feel more at peace and calm with what was happening. I had more understanding, and I felt lighter. And I thought, *Wow – this actually works!*

I know – I really, truly know – how hard it can be to start on a journey of taking care of yourself when you still feel that you're not worth being taken care of. But here's the thing: if you don't do it, no one else will. Here's another: YOU ARE WORTHY.

You are worthy of love.

You are worthy of happiness.

You are worthy of the best possible life you can make for yourself.

Yes, it may be hard to do, and it may seem as though that life is a really long way away from where you are now. But it's there for the making. I know it. I think you know it too. Always remember: *Your past does not define your future. You have everything you need within you.*

Here are a few last words from Kristine:

I see you. You are enough, just as you are. Right here, right now. Believe in yourself and trust your journey. You are exactly where you are meant to be.

If you need a short, snappy motivation, don't forget the one I use every day – I say it to myself, I say it out loud, I write it in my journal: I AM A GODDESS.

So are you.

Believe it.

Acknowledgements

Many thanks to Sophie and the dedicated team at Hachette Australia for believing in us and our vision to shine some much-needed light on mental health.

Sam Frost first came to public attention when she 'won' the second season of *The Bachelor.* She later became Australia's first Bachelorette, and for the last few years played the role of Jasmine on *Home and Away.* Recently, with her sister, Kristine, Sam launched BELIEVE by Sam Frost, an initiative for young girls and women that shines a much-needed light on mental health – focusing on depression, anxiety, toxic relationships and navigating the sometimes challenging world of social media.

Kristine Ross is a qualified youth mentor, fitness instructor, children's yoga teacher, and a mum of two daughters. She is the Founder and Director of Stronger – by BELIEVE, the sister organisation of BELIEVE by Sam Frost, whose programs help guide young girls to discover their own special qualities, and give them the tools to become compassionate and confident young women.

If you would like to find out more about Hachette Australia, our authors, upcoming events and new releases you can visit our website or our social media channels:

hachette.com.au

HachetteAustralia

HachetteAus